I0464231

How to Start a Nonprofit (and Actually Succeed!)

A Step-by-Step Guide for Visionaries and Changemakers

Matthew B. Scraper

Disclaimers and Copyright Information

ISBN 978-1-300-75333-9
Imprint: Lulu.com

Publisher Information

Published by Lulu Press, Inc.
For more information, visit **www.lulu.com**.

Disclaimer

The information provided in this book is based on the author's personal experiences, research, and professional expertise. While every effort has been made to ensure accuracy and relevance, this book is not intended as legal, financial, or professional advice. Readers are encouraged to seek appropriate counsel for their specific circumstances.

Acknowledgments

The author has made every effort to acknowledge and credit all sources and references used in this book. Any omissions or errors are unintentional and will be corrected in future editions, if notified.

Trademarks

All trademarks, service marks, product names, or named features mentioned in this book are the property of their respective owners. Use of these names does not imply any affiliation or endorsement.

Contact Information

For inquiries, permissions, or additional resources, visit **www.mbsoperations.com**.

First Edition

Printed in the United States of America.

Table of Contents

Contents

Introduction

The Purpose of This Book

Starting a nonprofit is more than a business decision—it's a calling. It's a response to a profound need, an answer to the inner pull to make a difference in the world. Unlike for-profit ventures driven by revenue and market share, nonprofits are fueled by mission, compassion, and a commitment to serve. This book recognizes that unique calling and seeks to guide you through every step of the journey with clarity and purpose.

Many founders are drawn to this path because of lived experiences, personal convictions, or a clear vision for social change. Whether you've been directly impacted by an issue or have identified an underserved community in need of support, your decision to start a nonprofit places you at the heart of transformational work. This book will not only validate that calling but also ensure you're equipped to pursue it with confidence.

By centering the heart of your mission, we'll help you establish a foundation that's rooted in ethical leadership, sustainable practices, and long-term impact. You'll be empowered to approach nonprofit creation as more than a paperwork process—it's a journey toward meaningful, measurable change.

What Readers Will Gain

If you've ever wondered how to translate your passion for social good into a structured, impactful organization, this book will provide you with the roadmap. You'll gain a comprehensive understanding of the steps required to launch a successful nonprofit from idea to implementation.

Here's what you can expect to learn:

- **Clear, Actionable Steps**: From conceptualizing your mission to filing for 501(c)(3) status, you'll receive step-by-step guidance that demystifies the process.

- **Real-Life Examples**: Learn from the experiences of successful nonprofit founders, their challenges, and how they overcame them.

- **Practical Tools and Templates**: Access checklists, templates, and sample documents that will simplify your path forward.

This book is designed to meet you where you are. Whether you're in the "I have an idea" phase or have already started piecing things together, the guidance here will give you the clarity to keep moving forward. No more guessing about IRS filings, bylaws, or board development—every section of this book is designed to offer practical support.

By the end of this book, you'll have a complete toolkit for nonprofit formation. You'll understand the "why" behind each step, not just the "how," equipping you to build an organization with integrity and sustainability at its core.

How This Book Fits into the Series

This book is the essential starting point in a broader series dedicated to nonprofit excellence. If you're familiar with my previous books on nonprofit operations, governance, and policy development, you'll see how this volume serves as the natural foundation for them all.

This approach is shaped by my insights and expertise as the founder of MBS Operations. As a seasoned Fractional COO, I bring a wealth of experience in nonprofit strategy, governance, and operational excellence. Through MBS Operations, I specialize in helping nonprofits and faith-based organizations strengthen their internal systems, improve governance, and achieve sustainable impact. Drawing from my experience as a former COO of the Oklahoma Center for Nonprofits, my military background, and my leadership within faith-based communities, I provide actionable guidance that empowers leaders to fulfill their mission with clarity and integrity. My expertise informs the principles, frameworks, and best practices presented throughout this book, ensuring you receive thoughtful, real-world advice at every step of the process.

Before you can effectively govern, manage operations, or establish policies, you need a nonprofit to lead. This book ensures you'll start on solid ground. It's a guide to building the infrastructure upon which everything else rests.

Other books in the series include:

1. **Effective Nonprofit Board Governance: Roles, Responsibilities, and Best Practices for Committees and Directors**

2. From the Pulpit to the Boardroom: How I Transitioned from a 20-Year Career in Ministry to the Nonprofit Sector

3. Policies and Procedures for Nonprofit Success: A Comprehensive Guide to Ethical and Effective Governance

4. The Nonprofit Operations Playbook: Strategic Operations for Mission-Driven Organizations

5. The Nonprofit Project Management Handbook: Deliver Projects that Drive Nonprofit Impact

6. Strategic and Tactical Planning for Nonprofits and Churches: A How-To Guide for Visionaries and Leaders

These works collectively offer a complete view of nonprofit leadership. While each book can stand alone, they are designed to support each other.

This book, *How to Start a Nonprofit (and Actually Succeed!): A Step-by-Step Guide for Visionaries and Changemakers*, gives you the firm footing you need before diving into more advanced areas like board governance, operational management, and policy development. By starting with this book, you'll be better prepared to lead with vision, navigate challenges, and sustain your organization's mission for the long term.

My Personal Journey

My path to nonprofit leadership was not linear. It started in the pulpit, not the boardroom. As an ordained elder in the

Oklahoma Indian Missionary Conference of the United Methodist Church, I've witnessed the power of faith-based communities to drive change. Ministry taught me about the human spirit—its struggles, its resilience, and its capacity for good. But I also learned hard lessons about structure, accountability, and sustainability.

When I transitioned from pastoral ministry to the nonprofit sector, I was surprised by how many of the same principles applied. Nonprofits and faith-based ministries both rely on shared values, servant leadership, and the ability to mobilize communities. But nonprofits have the added pressure of financial oversight, compliance, and growth management—all areas where I've seen organizations stumble.

I've been fortunate to lead operations at organizations like Faith in Public Life and the Oklahoma Center for Nonprofits, where I've seen firsthand the difference that strong operational systems can make. From onboarding and strategic planning to crisis management and policy development, every nonprofit faces these challenges. At Faith in Public Life, I've helped craft policies to protect staff from harassment and ensure compliance with employment law. At the Oklahoma Center for Nonprofits, I led our Standards for Excellence accreditation, solidifying my belief that clear standards are essential for success.

These experiences inspired me to write this book. I've seen too many founders overwhelmed by passion but undone by a lack of structure. I've seen nonprofit leaders with grand visions but no operational plan. I've seen good people make avoidable mistakes. This book is for them. It's for the pastor who feels called to address food insecurity but doesn't know where to start. It's for the community leader with a vision for change but no roadmap for execution.

I'm sharing these lessons because I've been in the trenches. I've had to revise financial reports at 3 AM before a board meeting. I've had to navigate HR crises and ethical dilemmas. I've had to face the reality that good intentions are not enough. Operations matter. Policies matter. Governance matters.

This book is not just a manual—it's a guide to help you avoid the mistakes I've seen too many nonprofits make. My hope is that you'll be able to navigate the complex world of nonprofit operations with confidence. Because starting a nonprofit isn't just about having a good idea—it's about having the right systems to sustain that idea for years to come.

Laying the Groundwork: Understanding What It Means to Start a Nonprofit

Starting a nonprofit organization is a journey that demands more than just passion for a cause. It requires a deep understanding of the landscape in which you will operate, strategic foresight, and the resilience to navigate a complex web of legal, financial, and operational requirements. Many aspiring founders begin with a vision of making a difference but quickly realize that good intentions alone are not enough.

Imagine standing at the base of a mountain, knowing you must climb to reach the peak where real impact can be made. The first steps in this journey are crucial, as they determine whether you will have the tools, support, and stamina to sustain your nonprofit over time. Before you file paperwork or launch a website, you need to establish a solid foundation—one built on clarity of purpose, a well-defined mission, and an understanding of the best structure for your organization.

This section will serve as your trusted guide, walking you through the foundational principles that will shape your nonprofit's trajectory. Whether you are just beginning to entertain the idea of launching a mission-driven organization or are already taking the first steps toward incorporation, these insights will provide clarity and direction. As you delve into these pages, you will gain a deeper understanding of the responsibilities, challenges, and rewards that come with leading a nonprofit. By the time you reach the end, you will not only have a clearer picture of what it truly means to start and sustain a nonprofit but also feel empowered with the knowledge and confidence to move forward with purpose and determination.

Defining Your Mission and Vision: The North Star for Your Nonprofit

Every successful nonprofit is built upon a well-defined mission and vision—these are the guiding stars that illuminate the path forward. Your mission acts as the heartbeat of your organization, articulating the fundamental purpose that drives your work each day. It answers the question: What change do we seek to create in the world? Meanwhile, your vision serves as a lighthouse in the distance, painting a picture of the world as it could be if your mission is realized. Together, they create a strong foundation, shaping your organization's strategic decisions, rallying support, and ensuring that every action taken aligns with your overarching purpose. Without a clear mission and vision, even the most well-intentioned efforts can lose direction in the complexities of nonprofit work.

- **Mission**: Your mission is the beating heart of your nonprofit—the core purpose that drives every initiative, decision, and action. It should be concise yet powerful, a statement that not only defines your organization's reason for existence but also inspires others to join in your cause. A well-crafted mission is action-oriented and specific, cutting through ambiguity to highlight the real-world impact your nonprofit strives to make.

14

Picture someone encountering your nonprofit for the first time—whether it's a donor, a volunteer, or a grant officer. In just a few words, your mission should answer their most pressing questions: "What problem are we solving, and for whom?"

A strong mission doesn't just describe what you do; it conveys the urgency of your work and the transformative change you aim to create. It is the foundation upon which your nonprofit will grow and thrive, shaping your programs, outreach, and strategic goals.

Example: "To provide after-school educational support and mentorship to underserved youth in rural communities."

- **Vision**: If the mission is the engine that propels your nonprofit forward, the vision is the destination on the horizon. It is the dream you are working toward, the world as it should be when your mission has been fully realized. A compelling vision is aspirational, expansive, and inspiring—offering a glimpse of a better future that others can rally behind.

Imagine the impact of your work stretched over years, perhaps even generations. What will change if your organization fulfills its mission? How will lives be transformed? A strong vision paints that picture, helping others see beyond the immediate efforts to the lasting legacy you hope to build.

A well-crafted vision statement serves not only as inspiration but also as a touchstone for decision-making, reminding your team and supporters why the work matters.

Whether you are eradicating hunger, ensuring access to education, or fighting for environmental justice, your vision should ignite passion and hope, serving as the North Star guiding every step of your nonprofit's journey.

Example: "A world where every child, regardless of location, has access to high-quality educational support and mentorship."

These elements will not only serve as your North Star, guiding every decision and action you take, but they will also be instrumental in securing funding, inspiring donor confidence, and shaping the strategic direction of your nonprofit. A well-crafted mission and vision will act as a powerful rallying cry, drawing in supporters, volunteers, and partners who resonate with your cause. Imagine standing before a room full of potential funders or collaborators—your ability to articulate a mission that is both compelling and heartfelt could mean the difference between gaining their support or losing their interest. Therefore, clarity, passion, and a deep sense of purpose should be infused into these guiding statements, ensuring they leave a lasting impact on all who encounter your organization.

Why Not Every Cause Needs a Nonprofit: Exploring Alternatives Before Committing

Before diving into the complex and rewarding world of nonprofit leadership, take a moment to step back and consider whether forming a nonprofit is truly the best path forward. While the idea of launching an organization dedicated to a cause you care about can be inspiring, it also comes with a significant commitment of time, financial resources, and ongoing legal responsibilities. Running a nonprofit isn't just about passion—it requires meticulous planning, regulatory compliance, and the ability to sustain operations over the long term. In some cases, alternative structures such as fiscal sponsorships or social enterprises may provide a more effective and less cumbersome route to achieving the same impact. Exploring these options early on can help ensure that your efforts are directed toward the most sustainable and impactful solution for your mission.

- **Fiscal Sponsorship**: If you have a powerful vision but lack the time, resources, or administrative expertise to start a nonprofit from scratch, fiscal sponsorship might be the perfect alternative. This arrangement allows you to align with an existing 501(c)(3) nonprofit that shares a similar mission, enabling you to operate under their tax-exempt status. By partnering with a fiscal sponsor, you gain access to critical infrastructure—such as grant funding opportunities, donor networks, and financial management support—without the immediate burden of establishing and maintaining your own organization.

Imagine being able to channel all your energy into the impact you want to create, rather than navigating the complex legal and financial requirements of nonprofit management. Whether you're launching a short-term project, testing the viability of a long-term initiative, or simply looking to make a difference as efficiently as possible, fiscal sponsorship provides a strategic pathway to bring your vision to life while leveraging the strength of an established organization.

Example: Instead of starting a new nonprofit focused on providing arts education, you could collaborate with a community arts center that's already established.

- **For-Profit Ventures with Social Impact**: In some cases, the best way to make a lasting impact isn't by forming a nonprofit but by creating a for-profit enterprise with a mission-driven focus. Social enterprises and benefit corporations (B Corps) blend purpose with profitability, allowing founders to generate revenue while advancing a cause. Unlike traditional nonprofits, these models provide greater flexibility in how they raise funds, distribute earnings, and structure operations.

Imagine an ethical fashion brand committed to sustainable manufacturing and fair wages. Instead of relying on donations or grants, the business generates revenue by selling high-quality products while promoting economic justice. Similarly, a tech company dedicated to making assistive technology more accessible can reinvest profits into product development, expanding its reach and social impact without being bound by the same restrictions nonprofits face.

By choosing this path, entrepreneurs can combine their passion for change with sustainable business practices, ensuring their mission is not just a side effort but embedded in the very foundation of their organization.

- **Community Partnerships**: Before setting out to build something new, take a step back and explore whether other organizations are already working toward a similar goal. Rather than reinventing the wheel, consider the power of collaboration. Partnering with an established nonprofit can provide access to existing resources, infrastructure, and community trust—key elements that often take years to develop from scratch.

By forming alliances, you can amplify your impact and reach a broader audience. Maybe your passion is increasing literacy rates, and there's already a local nonprofit offering tutoring services. Instead of creating a new program, you could strengthen theirs by providing additional volunteers, funding, or outreach. These types of partnerships not only prevent unnecessary duplication of efforts but also create a more unified and effective movement toward shared objectives.

True change is rarely achieved in isolation. By forging strong community partnerships, you can create a network of organizations working in harmony, each contributing unique strengths to a common cause.

Take time to carefully evaluate these alternatives before making the commitment to launch a nonprofit. While the idea of establishing and leading your own organization may be exciting and deeply fulfilling, it also comes with significant responsibilities that can quickly become overwhelming if you are unprepared. Managing a nonprofit extends far beyond a heartfelt mission—it requires navigating complex legal requirements, securing sustainable funding, managing operations, and ensuring ongoing compliance with state and federal regulations. If you find yourself drawn more to the cause than the organizational logistics, it might be worth considering whether collaboration with an existing nonprofit or another structure could allow you to make an even greater impact with fewer barriers. Thoughtfully weighing these options will help ensure that your passion is channeled into the most effective and sustainable path forward.

Legal Definitions and Types of Nonprofits: Understanding 501(c) Organizations

Nonprofits are not a one-size-fits-all structure. The IRS recognizes several types of 501(c) nonprofit organizations, each with different tax benefits, restrictions, and purposes. Choosing the right designation is critical to ensuring your nonprofit aligns with its intended activities and legal obligations.

- **501(c)(3) Public Charities and Private Foundations**: These nonprofits are established for charitable, educational, scientific, or religious purposes. They're eligible for tax-deductible donations and can receive grants from foundations and government agencies. However, they face strict limits on lobbying and political activities.

- o   Example: A food pantry that provides meals to homeless individuals would likely seek 501(c)(3) status to maximize donations from the public and foundations.
- **501(c)(4) Social Welfare Organizations**: While 501(c)(4) organizations also promote social welfare, they're allowed to engage in lobbying and advocacy work. Donations to 501(c)(4)s are not tax-deductible, but they have greater flexibility to participate in political activities.
  - o   Example: An advocacy group working to influence legislation on climate change might opt for 501(c)(4) status to engage in direct lobbying.
- **501(c)(5) Labor and Agricultural Organizations**: These nonprofits focus on improving labor conditions, agriculture, and horticulture. While contributions to these groups are not tax-deductible, they play a significant role in worker advocacy and collective bargaining.
  - o   Example: A farmer's uion dedicated to advocating for better wages and working conditions for agricultural workers.
- **501(c)(6) Trade and Professional Associations**: Organizations under this designation promote business interests and trade. These groups often support industries through networking, lobbying, and industry standards development.
  - o   Example: A local chamber of commerce that provides business development

resources and lobbies for pro-business policies.

- **501(c)(7) Social and Recreational Clubs**: These nonprofits operate for the pleasure, recreation, and social engagement of their members. Unlike other 501(c) organizations, these clubs do not primarily serve the public interest.
  - Example: A community yacht club that exists for the benefit of its paying members.
- **501(c)(8) and 501(c)(10) Fraternal Organizations**: These organizations provide social and charitable benefits to their members and communities. The difference between the two is that 501(c)(8) groups operate under a lodge system, while 501(c)(10) groups do not.
  - Example: A fraternal order that raises funds for scholarships and community service projects.
- **501(c)(19) Veterans' Organizations**: These nonprofits serve veterans and their families through services, advocacy, and community engagement.
  - Example: A nonprofit providing mental health support to veterans transitioning to civilian life.

While these are some of the most commonly recognized nonprofit types, the IRS has additional 501(c) classifications for specialized organizations. It's essential to select the designation that aligns with your organization's mission and long-term goals. Understanding the legal requirements of each type will help ensure compliance and sustainability for your nonprofit.

How Your Story Matters: Incorporating Your Personal Journey into the Purpose of the Organization

Every founder's story is unique, a tapestry woven with personal experiences, challenges, and triumphs that ultimately shape the mission of their nonprofit. Sharing this story does more than provide background; it breathes life into the organization, making it relatable and inspiring for those who encounter it.

When you allow people to see the journey that led you to start your nonprofit—whether it was a defining moment of struggle, an experience that opened your eyes to an unmet need, or a lifelong passion that evolved into a purpose-driven mission—you create an emotional connection that transcends facts and figures. People don't just support organizations; they support people and the causes that resonate with their own values and experiences.

Imagine a donor listening to your story and seeing their own experiences reflected in it, realizing that your nonprofit is a conduit for the change they also wish to see in the world. When stakeholders understand *why* you took this path, they become more than just supporters; they become champions of your mission, investing in the heart and soul of the cause alongside you.

- **Personal Experiences**: Your personal journey is often the catalyst for the mission you choose to pursue. Every nonprofit leader has a story—an experience that opened their eyes to an issue, a challenge they personally overcame, or an injustice

23

they witnessed that left an indelible mark. This journey forms the foundation of your nonprofit's work, making it more than just an abstract mission statement but a deeply personal commitment to change.

Think about what moments in your life shaped your understanding of the cause you now champion. Maybe you grew up in a food-insecure household, where you felt the sting of hunger firsthand. The memories of empty kitchen shelves, the reliance on food banks, and the community members who stepped in to help became defining elements of your story. This lived experience fuels your passion and gives your nonprofit a sense of authenticity that resonates with others.

When sharing your personal experiences, use storytelling to connect with your audience. Describe the emotions, the turning points, and the reasons why you felt compelled to take action. These narratives create a bridge between you and your supporters, transforming them from passive observers to active participants in your cause. By grounding your mission in real-life experiences, you invite others to see not only the problem but also the humanity behind it, making your nonprofit's work deeply relatable and inspiring.

- **Emotional Appeal**: At the heart of every successful nonprofit is a deeply personal story—one that sparks passion, commitment, and a sense of urgency. People connect with people, not organizations, which is why your personal journey is the most powerful tool in inspiring others to support your cause. Think back to the pivotal moment that led you to take action. Was it a single life-changing experience, a profound conversation, or a gradual realization that you could no longer ignore an issue close to your heart?

Perhaps it was an encounter with someone whose story mirrored your own struggles, or a moment of clarity that made you realize you had the power to make a difference. Whatever it was, that moment is the heart of your nonprofit's origin story, the 'why' behind your decision to dedicate your time and energy to a greater cause. When you share that story with honesty and emotion, you don't just describe your mission—you invite others to see the world through your eyes, to feel the urgency of your cause, and to step forward in solidarity.

Your ability to communicate the depth of your passion can transform passive listeners into active supporters, whether they are donors, volunteers, or advocates for your mission. By grounding your nonprofit in a compelling, personal narrative, you create a movement driven not just by purpose, but by the human connections that fuel lasting change.

- **Values-Driven Leadership**: Leadership in the nonprofit sector isn't just about strategy and execution; it's about embodying the values that drive your mission. Your personal beliefs and principles should be more than just words on a website—they should be the foundation of your organization's culture, decision-making, and impact.

If equity and justice fuel your passion, these values should be reflected in every aspect of your nonprofit, from hiring practices to program design and stakeholder engagement. Leadership rooted in values fosters trust, cultivates community, and ensures your organization stays true to its purpose, even in challenging times.

Consider how your personal journey has shaped your perspective on leadership. Maybe you come from a background where you witnessed systemic inequities firsthand, and that experience informs your approach to advocacy. Or perhaps your faith, upbringing, or professional experiences instilled in you a commitment to service and integrity. When you weave these values into the fabric of your nonprofit, they become more than ideals—they become a living, breathing part of your organization's identity.

Example: In my own journey from ministry to nonprofit leadership, I've seen firsthand how values like compassion, service, and justice shape the work we do. These principles guide not only the programs we run but also how we engage with staff, volunteers, and the communities we serve. Values-driven leadership is not just a framework—it's a commitment to making decisions that align with the deeper purpose behind your mission.

When you weave your personal story into the very fabric of your nonprofit's purpose, you transform your organization into something more than just a mission statement—you create a brand that is deeply authentic, transparent, and profoundly relatable. People don't just support causes;

they support individuals whose passion and experiences resonate with them on a human level.

Your story serves as the emotional bridge that connects supporters to your cause. It provides depth, meaning, and relatability, allowing donors, volunteers, and partners to see themselves in your journey. Whether it's the pivotal moment that inspired your nonprofit's inception, the personal challenges that shaped your commitment to your cause, or the triumphs that reaffirm why this work matters, sharing your story makes your organization more than an entity—it makes it a movement.

By incorporating your narrative into your fundraising campaigns, marketing efforts, and recruitment strategies, you invite people into your mission in a way that statistics and impact reports alone cannot achieve. A compelling story evokes empathy, inspires action, and fosters loyalty, ensuring that those who believe in you will stand beside you in your efforts to create meaningful change.

Conclusion

Laying the groundwork for a nonprofit is not just about paperwork and planning—it's about shaping a vision that will guide your journey for years to come. This process requires deep reflection, thorough research, and strategic foresight to ensure your organization is set up for long-term success.

At the core of this foundation is your mission and vision, serving as a beacon that directs every decision and initiative your nonprofit undertakes. These elements don't just outline what you do; they inspire action, create a sense of purpose, and rally supporters around a shared goal. Before you take the formal steps to incorporate your nonprofit, it's essential to evaluate whether launching your own organization is the right move. Exploring alternatives, such as fiscal sponsorship or social enterprises, can sometimes be a more efficient way to bring your vision to life without taking on the administrative and financial burdens of running a new entity.

Understanding the different types of nonprofit designations is another crucial step in this journey. Choosing the right legal structure ensures compliance with regulatory requirements, enables you to maximize fundraising opportunities, and helps protect your mission's integrity.

Finally, beyond the technical aspects of forming a nonprofit, there is the deeply personal element: your story. Every successful nonprofit is born from a place of passion, often tied to the founder's personal experiences, struggles, and triumphs. Sharing that journey adds authenticity, emotional depth, and credibility to your mission, making it more relatable to donors, volunteers, and the community you serve.

By thoughtfully engaging with these foundational concepts, you'll be equipped to launch a nonprofit that isn't just impactful in the short term but is built to sustain and thrive for years to come.

Research and Planning

Embarking on the journey of launching a nonprofit is akin to setting sail into uncharted waters. It requires more than just good intentions—it demands a compass of research and a map of strategic planning. Passion and purpose may provide the wind in your sails, but without direction and careful navigation, even the most well-intentioned efforts can drift off course.

Imagine standing at the threshold of a new endeavor, driven by a deep desire to make a difference. Before you take the first step, it is essential to look around, understand the landscape, and ask fundamental questions: What are the pressing needs of the community? How will your nonprofit bring something unique to the table? And perhaps most importantly, can your vision be sustained financially in the long run?

This stage of research and planning is about building a sturdy foundation—one that will not only support your organization's mission but also ensure its longevity. Below, we will explore the crucial steps that will transform your vision into a well-grounded, impactful nonprofit, ready to serve and thrive.

1. Conducting a Needs Assessment

Every great nonprofit begins with a question: What problem are we trying to solve? At the heart of every successful nonprofit lies a deep understanding of the community it serves. A needs assessment is more than just a checklist—

it's an opportunity to engage with people, hear their stories, and understand their struggles. It helps uncover the gaps that existing services fail to address and ensures that your nonprofit's mission is not just well-intentioned, but absolutely necessary.

Imagine walking through the neighborhood you hope to serve. You talk to local families, community leaders, and business owners. They share their experiences—their frustrations, their hopes, their unmet needs. Some may tell you about a lack of job training programs, while others speak about food insecurity or access to affordable childcare. As you listen, patterns emerge. You begin to see where existing programs fall short and where your nonprofit can step in to make a tangible difference.

A needs assessment isn't just about collecting data; it's about gaining insight. It allows you to identify not just what is lacking, but why. It helps you refine your mission and align your efforts with the actual needs of the community, rather than assumptions. By approaching this step with curiosity and a commitment to truly understanding the people you wish to serve, you lay the foundation for a nonprofit that is both impactful and sustainable.

Here's how you can approach this critical step:

a. Gather Data

Imagine stepping into a community meeting, the hum of conversation filling the air as people share their experiences, concerns, and aspirations. Conducting a needs assessment is about more than just collecting numbers—it's about listening, truly hearing the voices of those who will be impacted by your work.

Surveys and questionnaires serve as valuable tools for capturing these voices, offering a structured way to gather input from potential beneficiaries, stakeholders, and local leaders. These can reveal patterns in need, priorities, and even innovative ideas from the very people your nonprofit aims to serve. But sometimes, a simple survey isn't enough to capture the depth of human experience.

To dig deeper, you might organize focus groups—small gatherings where individuals can discuss the challenges they face in their daily lives. Imagine sitting in a circle, hearing firsthand from single parents about childcare barriers, from young professionals about job training struggles, or from elders about the isolation they endure. These discussions provide rich, qualitative data that numbers alone cannot convey.

Beyond direct conversations, there's a wealth of existing information that can inform your understanding. Public data sources such as census reports, community health assessments, and government studies offer a broad perspective on demographic trends, economic shifts, and pressing social issues. These can help validate your findings, revealing the full scope of the problem you're addressing.

For an even more personal insight, consider one-on-one interviews with key community leaders, nonprofit executives, and long-time residents. These individuals have a pulse on the needs of the area, often recognizing patterns and gaps that large datasets might overlook. Their perspectives can guide your approach, ensuring your nonprofit not only meets an identified need but does so in a way that resonates with the community.

In the end, gathering data is about blending statistics with stories, using both empirical evidence and human experience to paint a complete picture of the need you're addressing. The more comprehensive your understanding, the stronger your foundation for building a nonprofit that truly makes a difference.

b. Analyze Existing Services

Picture yourself stepping into a bustling town square where various organizations, nonprofits, and agencies have set up booths, each offering a different kind of support to the community. Some focus on food insecurity, others on housing, education, or mental health services. As you weave through the space, you begin to notice something— certain needs appear to be well covered, while others seem barely addressed. This is precisely the kind of observation you must make when analyzing the nonprofit landscape around you.

Understanding the ecosystem of existing services is essential. It prevents duplication of efforts and allows you to strategically position your nonprofit to fill gaps rather than compete for the same resources. Start by mapping out who is already working in your space. Are there established organizations, government initiatives, or community groups tackling similar issues? If so, what approaches are they using? Are there particular demographics they serve while others remain underserved?

As you dig deeper, you may notice overlaps—organizations working toward similar goals but perhaps not in a coordinated fashion. You may also uncover glaring service gaps, such as a program for at-risk youth that provides mentorship but lacks job training opportunities. Your role is to identify where your nonprofit can add value rather than simply replicate existing work.

Analyzing existing services isn't just about research—it's about engagement. Reach out to leaders of these organizations, attend community meetings, and speak with beneficiaries who rely on these programs. Their insights can reveal inefficiencies, unmet needs, and areas ripe for collaboration. By developing a clear understanding of the nonprofit landscape, you position your organization to be a complementary force, ensuring resources are distributed where they are needed most.

This step is not only practical but strategic. Funders, stakeholders, and community members will be more likely to support your nonprofit if they see that it serves a unique, necessary role rather than competing with existing services. By conducting a thorough analysis, you build credibility and lay the groundwork for meaningful partnerships, ultimately making your nonprofit more impactful and sustainable.

c. Identify the Core Needs

After gathering and analyzing the data, the next step is to sharpen your focus on the essential issues that demand attention. Picture yourself standing in the middle of the community you wish to serve. What do you see? Are there families struggling with food insecurity, but no nearby pantry? Are there young adults eager for employment opportunities, yet no accessible job training programs?

Your goal is to identify these unmet needs with clarity and precision. Are particular demographics being left behind— perhaps single parents, the elderly, or recent immigrants? Are there specific geographic areas that remain underserved due to a lack of transportation or infrastructure? By drilling down into the details, you ensure that your nonprofit's work will make a tangible difference where it is needed most.

This is the moment where your vision transforms from a broad idea into a clear and actionable mission. Take what you have learned from your research, conversations, and observations, and use it to paint a vivid picture of the problem you are trying to solve. The clearer you can define these core needs, the stronger your foundation for building meaningful, lasting change.

d. Document Findings

Your journey of discovery has led you to a wealth of insights, stories, and data. Now comes the pivotal step of capturing those findings in a way that informs and inspires. Think of this document as the blueprint for your nonprofit—it will guide decision-making, define your mission and goals, and serve as a touchstone for your work moving forward.

Creating a formal report isn't just about listing statistics; it's about weaving together the voices you've heard, the data you've analyzed, and the urgent needs you've identified. This document should tell a compelling story—one that paints a clear picture of the community's challenges while also highlighting the gaps your nonprofit seeks to fill.

Your findings will also be invaluable when engaging potential funders. A well-structured report demonstrates not only the tangible need for your organization but also your commitment to addressing it with informed, strategic action. Funders want to see evidence that your nonprofit is based on research rather than assumption, and this document provides the proof they need to invest in your cause.

Consider breaking your report into clear sections: an executive summary for quick reference, a detailed needs assessment, an analysis of existing services, and a final section outlining the key areas your nonprofit will address. Use visuals, quotes, and real-life examples to bring your findings to life. The stronger and clearer this document is, the more effectively it will guide your nonprofit toward meaningful, lasting impact.

2. Defining Your Unique Value Proposition

In a world overflowing with charitable organizations, standing out is more than a matter of branding—it's about finding and articulating your nonprofit's true purpose in a way that resonates. Your Unique Value Proposition (UVP) is not just a statement; it is the heartbeat of your organization, the essence that differentiates you from the sea of good intentions. Imagine walking into a room full of passionate changemakers, all advocating for noble causes—what makes your nonprofit distinct? Why should a donor choose to support you over another? Why will the community turn to you rather than an existing organization?

Your UVP is the answer to these questions. It is the bold declaration of your nonprofit's identity, its purpose distilled into a clear and compelling message. Defining your UVP is not merely an exercise in differentiation—it's about ensuring that your mission is necessary, your approach is impactful, and your voice is heard above the noise. Here's how to craft a UVP that doesn't just inform but inspires:

a. Identify Your Core Competencies

Think about what makes your nonprofit not just another organization, but a vital force for change. Every successful nonprofit has a distinctive approach, an area of expertise that sets it apart. What will your nonprofit do better than anyone else? What unique skills, experiences, or methodologies do you bring to the table?

Imagine yourself at a conference filled with nonprofit leaders and funders. You're asked to stand up and share, in just a few sentences, why your nonprofit is different. What would you say? Perhaps your team has years of experience in trauma-informed care, equipping you to support survivors in a way others cannot. Maybe you've developed a groundbreaking curriculum that helps children in underserved communities excel academically. Your core competencies are not just about what you do—they're about how and why you do it in a way no one else can replicate.

To define your core competencies, reflect on the strengths of your leadership team, the innovative strategies you employ, and the specialized knowledge you have. Your goal is not just to be effective, but to be exceptional in a way that inspires confidence and support from funders, stakeholders, and the community you serve.

b. Highlight the Unique Benefits of Your Services

Imagine sitting across from a potential donor or a community leader, eager to share why your nonprofit exists. What is the first thing you would say? Would you talk about the people whose lives will be transformed because of your work? Would you describe the ripple effect of change that begins with just one initiative, reaching far beyond what you initially envisioned?

Your nonprofit is more than just an organization—it's a catalyst for meaningful, lasting change. The work you do should not only meet immediate needs but also create a sustainable impact. Will you serve an underserved population, ensuring that forgotten voices are finally heard? Will you address a long-overlooked issue, bringing fresh solutions where none existed before?

By clearly defining the change you seek to create, you make it easier for donors, supporters, and community members to see why your nonprofit matters. People connect with stories, and your organization's unique benefits should be framed in a way that resonates emotionally and intellectually. Show them not just what you do, but why it matters—why it's the missing piece in the broader puzzle of social change. The stronger your case, the more support you will inspire.

c. Analyze Competitors

Imagine stepping into a vibrant marketplace where every booth represents a nonprofit working toward a similar cause. Each has its own story, strategy, and approach, yet despite their efforts, gaps remain—needs still go unmet, and opportunities for improvement abound. To carve out your own space and make a meaningful impact, you must take a close, thoughtful look at these fellow organizations. What makes them successful? What do they do exceptionally well that has earned them trust, funding, and effectiveness?

Beyond admiration, critical thinking is required. What is missing from their approach that you can offer? Perhaps they have broad programs but lack personalization. Maybe they focus on one demographic but overlook another equally in need. Or it could be that they have an outdated model, and your innovative methods can bridge the gap.

This analysis isn't about competition—it's about contribution. By deeply understanding where others excel and where they falter, you can position your nonprofit not as an alternative but as an essential complement to existing services. This strategic positioning ensures that your nonprofit doesn't duplicate efforts but instead fills crucial gaps, making your organization a truly valuable new player in the space.

d. Create a Clear and Compelling Statement

Once you've identified your unique advantages, it's time to distill them into a statement that is not only clear but also emotionally resonant and inspiring. Think of your Unique Value Proposition (UVP) as your nonprofit's rallying cry— the succinct message that captures the essence of your work and makes people sit up and take notice.

Your UVP should tell a story in just a few sentences. It should highlight the problem you are addressing, the people you are serving, and the innovative approach that sets you apart. Imagine yourself in an elevator with a potential donor or community leader—you have just 30 seconds to convey why your nonprofit exists and why it matters. What would you say?

Consider this example: "We provide trauma-informed mentorship for foster youth aged 14-18, preparing them for higher education and employment opportunities that other local nonprofits do not offer. Through personalized support and skill-building, we empower young people to break cycles of instability and create their own success stories."

Your UVP should evoke a sense of urgency, purpose, and the promise of tangible impact. It should make funders, volunteers, and community members want to learn more— and, most importantly, take action to support your mission.

e. Test Your UVP

Your Unique Value Proposition is not something to craft in solitude and then set in stone—it's a living, evolving message that should be refined through conversation and experience. Imagine gathering a group of trusted partners, board members, and funders around a table, presenting your UVP, and watching their reactions. Are their eyes lighting up with understanding and enthusiasm, or do they seem uncertain about your nonprofit's distinction? Their feedback is invaluable.

Testing your UVP is like fine-tuning a powerful speech. It should be clear, compelling, and resonate deeply with those who hear it. Engage in discussions with people who believe in your mission and those who challenge it. Ask tough questions: Does this statement truly capture our essence? Does it clearly convey why our nonprofit is different? Would a donor feel inspired to support us after hearing this?

Use this process not only to sharpen your message but also to deepen your understanding of how others perceive your organization. When your UVP is strong, it will serve as a guiding light—illuminating your path forward and drawing others into your mission with clarity and conviction.

3. Researching Funding Availability

Every dream, no matter how noble, needs a foundation of financial support to turn vision into reality. Picture a newly planted tree—it requires water, sunlight, and rich soil to grow strong and bear fruit. Similarly, a nonprofit must cultivate diverse funding sources to sustain its mission and make a lasting impact. Before you launch your organization, it's crucial to map out where your financial resources will come from and how you'll ensure long-term sustainability. Without a solid funding strategy, even the most passionate initiatives can struggle to survive. Here's how to approach this vital task with foresight and strategy:

a. Identify Potential Revenue Streams

Imagine a nonprofit as a thriving ecosystem, sustained by a variety of resources working in harmony. Just as a river is fed by multiple streams, a successful nonprofit must diversify its funding sources to ensure stability and growth. Relying solely on one type of funding is like depending on a single well—when it runs dry, the entire organization suffers. Diversification not only mitigates financial risk but also broadens the reach of your mission.

Consider the many paths through which your nonprofit can generate revenue. Grants from foundations, corporations, and government agencies offer substantial support, but they are often highly competitive and come with specific requirements. Individual donations—whether through one-time gifts, crowdfunding campaigns, or recurring monthly contributions—can provide a more flexible and sustainable income stream. Picture a community of dedicated supporters, each contributing a small amount that collectively fuels impactful programs year after year.

Beyond donations, some nonprofits find success in generating revenue by offering paid services or selling mission-aligned products. Whether it's hosting educational workshops, providing consulting services, or selling handmade goods that support artisan communities, these earned-income strategies can reinforce financial independence. Additionally, partnerships with corporations can unlock sponsorship opportunities, employee giving programs, and in-kind donations that reduce operational costs.

By carefully crafting a diverse funding portfolio, your nonprofit can build resilience, ensuring that financial setbacks in one area do not jeopardize your ability to serve the community. As you explore these revenue streams, keep in mind that sustainability is not just about securing funds—it's about creating a network of supporters, investors, and partners who believe in your vision and contribute to its long-term success.

b. Conduct a Fundability Assessment

Imagine standing at the crossroads of passion and practicality, asking yourself one crucial question: Is my cause fundable? The reality is that not all nonprofit missions attract equal levels of financial support. Some causes—like education, health, and environmental conservation—naturally align with large-scale grant funding and philanthropic interest, while others require creative strategies to secure long-term sustainability.

To assess your mission's fundability, take a deep dive into the funding landscape. Explore reports from major foundations, government agencies, and corporate giving programs to identify which sectors receive the most financial backing. Study nonprofits with similar missions to see how they sustain themselves—what grantmakers fund them? Do they rely heavily on individual donors, earned revenue, or corporate partnerships?

Beyond research, engage with potential funders directly. Attend nonprofit conferences, reach out to grant officers for guidance, and participate in funding workshops to better understand what funders look for. Remember, fundability isn't just about finding available money—it's about aligning your mission with the priorities of those willing to invest in change. By carefully evaluating your cause's financial landscape, you can position your nonprofit for long-term success and avoid the pitfalls of underfunding.

c. Assess Initial Funding Needs

Picture yourself at the helm of your nonprofit, ready to embark on your mission, but first, you must determine the financial fuel needed to keep it moving forward. Just as a builder would never construct a home without estimating material costs, you must carefully outline the expenses required to launch and sustain your organization.

Start with the foundational costs. How much money will you need to get your nonprofit off the ground? Consider legal fees for incorporation, branding and marketing efforts to spread awareness, and initial staffing to ensure your organization runs smoothly. Then, think beyond the launch—what are the recurring expenses that will keep your nonprofit thriving year after year? Rent, utilities, program expenses, salaries, technology, and insurance all play a crucial role in long-term sustainability.

By painting a detailed financial picture, you'll not only set realistic fundraising goals but also build credibility with potential funders. No donor or grant provider wants to invest in an organization that hasn't thought through its financial viability. The more clarity and precision you bring to this assessment, the stronger your case for support will be, ensuring your nonprofit has the resources needed to make a meaningful and lasting impact.

d. Build a Funding Strategy

Creating a funding strategy is like assembling the financial blueprint of your nonprofit's future. It requires foresight, adaptability, and a deep understanding of how to cultivate resources that will sustain your mission over time. A successful funding plan is not built on wishful thinking but on a solid framework that outlines how your organization will attract and maintain financial support.

Imagine a nonprofit that relies solely on one major grant. At first, everything runs smoothly—programs are launched, staff is hired, and services reach those in need. But then, the grant expires or is not renewed, and suddenly, the organization is scrambling to keep its doors open. To avoid this precarious situation, it is essential to diversify your funding sources.

A strong funding strategy includes multiple revenue streams, such as grant applications to foundations and government agencies, individual donor campaigns, corporate sponsorships, and earned income through service fees or product sales. It also considers long-term sustainability—developing recurring donation programs, legacy giving opportunities, and fundraising events that create lasting financial resilience.

Building relationships is just as critical as securing funds. Engaging with donors, grant officers, and corporate sponsors before seeking financial support can strengthen your credibility and increase the likelihood of funding success. A well-thought-out strategy ensures that no single funding source holds the fate of your nonprofit in its hands, allowing you to focus on your mission rather than financial uncertainty.

e. Engage Funders Early

Building relationships with funders should never be an afterthought—it should be a cornerstone of your nonprofit's financial strategy. Imagine stepping into a room of potential supporters, each holding the key to resources that could help bring your mission to life. The challenge is not just securing their support but fostering connections that go beyond transactional funding.

Don't wait until you're ready to submit a grant application to make introductions. Funders are more likely to invest in organizations they know and trust, so take proactive steps to establish rapport early. Attend community events where grant officers and corporate sponsors gather. Seek opportunities to engage in meaningful conversations, not just about your funding needs, but about shared values and long-term impact.

Informational meetings with potential funders can serve as invaluable learning opportunities. Instead of simply pitching your nonprofit, ask thoughtful questions—what projects excite them? What are their biggest concerns when considering grant applications? Demonstrating curiosity and adaptability can make funders feel like partners rather than just financial backers.

By cultivating these relationships early, you position your nonprofit as a credible, mission-driven organization that funders want to champion. When the time comes to submit a grant or funding request, your proposal will land on the desk of someone who already understands and believes in your work.

f. Test Your Funding Assumptions

The best way to determine whether your funding strategy will stand the test of time is to put it into action. Think of this step as a trial run—an opportunity to validate your financial approach before committing to long-term investments. Launching a pilot program not only allows you to gauge interest and secure initial funding but also offers tangible proof that your nonprofit can deliver meaningful impact.

Imagine announcing your pilot initiative to the community. Will people rally around your cause? Will donors step forward to provide financial backing? These early responses provide invaluable insights into the feasibility of your broader fundraising strategy. A well-executed pilot allows you to collect data, refine your messaging, and build momentum before scaling up your efforts.

Moreover, pilot programs create compelling narratives. Every small success—every individual helped, every milestone achieved—becomes a story you can share with potential funders. These stories transform abstract proposals into real-world proof, making grant applications, donor pitches, and sponsorship requests far more persuasive.

Testing your funding assumptions isn't about ensuring perfection from the start—it's about learning, adapting, and proving that your nonprofit has both the vision and the viability to thrive in the long run.

Conclusion

Launching a nonprofit is more than just a leap of faith—it's a deliberate, strategic process that transforms passion into tangible impact. Think of it as constructing a bridge: passion serves as the spark that fuels your ambition, but without careful planning, thorough research, and a clear roadmap, your vision may never reach the other side.

By conducting a needs assessment, you ensure that your nonprofit is built on real, pressing community challenges rather than assumptions. By defining your unique value proposition, you carve out a distinct space in an already crowded landscape of charitable organizations, ensuring that your work stands out. And by researching funding availability, you lay the financial groundwork that will sustain your mission for years to come.

With this foundation in place, you can move forward with confidence, knowing that your nonprofit is not just a dream but a well-planned, sustainable force for good. You are not just hoping to make a difference—you are preparing to make one, equipped with knowledge, strategy, and a commitment to meaningful change.

Legal Formation and Registration

Embarking on the journey to start a nonprofit organization is a thrilling yet intricate endeavor that requires more than just a passion for a cause—it demands strategic planning, diligence, and a deep commitment to fulfilling legal obligations. This process is not merely about completing paperwork; it is about creating a sturdy foundation upon which your organization will stand, one that ensures longevity and effectiveness in serving its mission. Every decision, from selecting a name that captures the essence of your work to structuring a governance system that fosters accountability and transparency, plays a crucial role in shaping your nonprofit's future.

Navigating the legal landscape can feel overwhelming at first, but each step serves a purpose in protecting your organization and solidifying its credibility. Incorporating your nonprofit not only provides legitimacy but also establishes it as a distinct legal entity, safeguarding it from unnecessary liabilities. Achieving tax-exempt status unlocks significant financial advantages, allowing your organization to receive tax-deductible donations and qualify for grant funding. Equally important is setting up a financial framework that ensures fiscal responsibility, helping you build trust with donors and stakeholders.

While the legal formalities may seem like obstacles, they are in fact stepping stones that lead to a strong and resilient organization. By methodically addressing each requirement, you are not just ensuring compliance—you are laying the groundwork for a nonprofit that can thrive, grow, and make a lasting impact in the community it seeks to serve. The road may be challenging, but with careful planning and dedication, your nonprofit will be well-positioned to bring its mission to life and create meaningful change.

1. The Legal Steps to Incorporate

The journey to bringing your nonprofit to life starts with one of the most critical steps—formal incorporation. This step is more than just a bureaucratic requirement; it establishes your nonprofit as a legitimate entity, providing legal protection and paving the way for tax-exempt status. Incorporation involves three essential actions: selecting a name, filing articles of incorporation, and drafting bylaws.

Your nonprofit's name is its identity, the first impression it will make on potential supporters, donors, and the community it serves. Choosing the right name is about more than creativity—it must be unique and reflective of your organization's mission. To avoid conflicts, check your state's Secretary of State website to ensure the name is available. In some states, you can even reserve the name for a small fee, ensuring that it remains yours while you complete the incorporation process.

Once you have secured a name, it's time to make it official by filing your articles of incorporation with the Secretary of State's office in the state where your nonprofit will be based. Think of this document as your nonprofit's birth certificate—it formally registers your organization as a legal entity. The articles include key details such as the nonprofit's name, purpose, principal office address, and the names of the initial board members. You'll also need to designate a registered agent, a person responsible for receiving legal notices on behalf of the organization. Filing fees for articles of incorporation vary widely by state, typically ranging from $50 to $400, so be sure to check with your state's specific requirements before submitting your paperwork.

With incorporation complete, the next step is drafting your bylaws—an essential document that will shape your nonprofit's operations and governance. Bylaws serve as the rulebook for how your nonprofit functions, outlining the roles and responsibilities of board members, defining voting procedures, and establishing guidelines for handling conflicts of interest. Well-crafted bylaws provide stability and clarity, ensuring that your nonprofit is equipped to navigate challenges and make decisions effectively. These bylaws must be formally adopted by the board during the first organizational meeting, a significant milestone that marks the transition from idea to operational entity.

Incorporation is not just a legal formality—it's the foundation upon which your nonprofit will be built. Taking the time to get this step right ensures that your organization is set up for long-term success, allowing you to focus on your mission with confidence.

2. Filing for 501(c)(3) Tax-Exempt Status

After successfully incorporating your nonprofit, the next crucial step is securing 501(c)(3) tax-exempt status from the IRS. This designation not only exempts your organization from federal income tax but also allows donors to make tax-deductible contributions, enhancing your fundraising potential. While the application process might seem overwhelming, breaking it into manageable steps makes it much more approachable.

First, take a moment to evaluate whether your organization's purpose aligns with the IRS's criteria for 501(c)(3) status. Nonprofits dedicated to charitable, religious, scientific, educational, or literary purposes typically qualify. If your mission fits within these categories, you can proceed to selecting the right IRS form. For organizations expecting gross receipts over $50,000 annually, Form 1023 is the standard application. However, smaller organizations that meet eligibility requirements may take advantage of Form 1023-EZ, a streamlined version designed for simplicity and quicker approval.

Before you start the application, you'll need to compile essential documents, including your articles of incorporation, bylaws, and a list of your board members. Additionally, the IRS requires a detailed narrative description of your organization's planned activities, along with projected financial statements. This section of the application is particularly important, as it helps the IRS assess whether your nonprofit genuinely serves a public interest and qualifies for tax exemption.

Once your documentation is in order, you can submit your application electronically through the IRS's Pay.gov system. The filing fees, which are $600 for Form 1023 and $275 for Form 1023-EZ, must be paid at the time of submission. After reviewing your application, the IRS may reach out with follow-up questions or requests for clarification. Once everything is in place, you will receive your IRS determination letter—a milestone that officially grants your nonprofit tax-exempt status and opens the door to expanded fundraising opportunities.

Achieving 501(c)(3) status is a significant step toward establishing credibility and sustainability for your nonprofit. With this designation in hand, your organization can confidently engage donors, apply for grants, and focus on advancing its mission with the reassurance that it meets all necessary legal and financial standards.

3. State-Specific Requirements

Each state has its own unique regulations governing nonprofits, making it crucial to thoroughly research your specific state's legal requirements. This research is essential for ensuring your organization remains compliant with all necessary laws, allowing it to operate smoothly and effectively. Typically, there are three major components to state compliance: registering for charitable solicitations, securing state tax exemptions, and fulfilling ongoing reporting requirements.

If your nonprofit intends to raise funds from the public, you will likely need to file a charitable solicitation registration with the state's attorney general or another regulatory agency. This process serves as a safeguard, ensuring transparency and accountability in how donations are collected and used. Depending on the state, the registration may need to be renewed annually, and some states require financial disclosures or audits to accompany these filings.

In addition to fundraising regulations, many states offer tax exemptions beyond the federal 501(c)(3) designation. These may include exemptions from state income tax, property tax, or even sales tax. However, each exemption requires a separate application and must meet the specific qualifications set by state law. Some states also require periodic renewals to maintain tax-exempt status, making it vital to keep track of filing deadlines and documentation requirements.

Finally, maintaining good standing with the state often involves submitting an annual or biennial report. This report typically includes basic organizational information, such as updated board member listings, financial summaries, and proof of ongoing compliance with state regulations. Failure to submit required reports can result in penalties or even loss of incorporation status, which can significantly hinder your nonprofit's operations.

Navigating state-specific requirements may seem daunting, but resources are available to simplify the process. Your state's Secretary of State website is an excellent place to start, as it provides official forms, deadlines, and detailed guidance on compliance. Additionally, organizations like the National Association of State Charity Officials (NASCO) at www.nasconet.org offer valuable insights into multi-state regulations and best practices for nonprofit compliance. By staying informed and proactive, your nonprofit can ensure smooth operations and maintain its legal standing for years to come.

4. Setting Up a Bank Account and EIN

A critical step in the financial foundation of your nonprofit is securing an Employer Identification Number (EIN) and setting up a dedicated bank account. These two elements are fundamental in keeping your nonprofit's finances distinct from personal funds, allowing the organization to properly manage donations, expenses, and operational costs while ensuring compliance with financial regulations.

Obtaining an EIN is a straightforward and free process, yet it is an essential component of your nonprofit's identity. Much like a Social Security number for individuals, an EIN serves as a unique identifier for your organization, required for tax filings, payroll, and banking. You can apply for an EIN directly through the IRS website, and in most cases, you will receive it immediately after completing the online application. Having an EIN not only legitimizes your nonprofit in the eyes of the IRS but also streamlines financial transactions, making grant applications and donor contributions easier to manage.

Once your nonprofit has an EIN, the next step is to establish a nonprofit-specific bank account. It's crucial to research financial institutions that offer low-cost or fee-free options tailored for nonprofits. Some banks provide specialized services, such as waived fees, access to donor management tools, or enhanced security for nonprofit

54

accounts. When opening the account, you will need to present several important documents, including your EIN, articles of incorporation, bylaws, and government-issued identification for individuals authorized to manage the account. Additionally, some banks may require a copy of your IRS determination letter, which confirms your organization's tax-exempt status.

Beyond merely opening a bank account, implementing sound financial controls from the start will set your nonprofit up for long-term stability. Consider establishing clear policies regarding check-signing authority, dual-approval processes for expenses, and the use of accounting software like QuickBooks or Xero to track finances. These internal controls help prevent financial mismanagement, maintain transparency, and build trust among donors, grantmakers, and stakeholders.

By taking these critical financial steps early on, your nonprofit will be well-positioned to operate efficiently, ensuring every dollar received is managed with integrity and accountability. This financial groundwork not only protects your organization but also reinforces the trust and confidence of those who support your mission.

By carefully navigating these legal steps, your nonprofit will emerge as a fully established, tax-exempt entity, poised to make a lasting impact. Incorporating your organization not only grants it official recognition but also provides legal protections and legitimacy that will help attract donors, partners, and grant funding. Securing tax-exempt status opens the doors to increased financial opportunities and allows your supporters to contribute with confidence, knowing their donations are tax-deductible. Ensuring compliance with state-specific regulations further strengthens your credibility, reassuring both the community you serve and those who invest in your mission.

With a solid legal and financial foundation in place, you can shift your focus from administrative processes to the heart of your nonprofit's work—creating meaningful change. Whether you are addressing urgent community needs, advancing social justice initiatives, or supporting education and the arts, your organization is now equipped with the structure and resources necessary to thrive. The journey to building a nonprofit is not always easy, but by approaching each step with intention and diligence, you have set the stage for lasting success. The work ahead will be rewarding, and with the right framework in place, your nonprofit can truly make a difference in the world.

Building Your Board of Directors

Introduction

Building an effective board of directors is the backbone of any successful nonprofit organization. More than just a governing body, the board serves as the steward of the organization's mission, ensuring that every decision made aligns with its core values and long-term goals. A strong board provides strategic guidance, financial oversight, and fiduciary accountability, but its role extends beyond these fundamental responsibilities. It is a team of passionate leaders dedicated to seeing the nonprofit thrive and expand its impact.

Each board member brings unique skills and perspectives that help shape the organization's direction. They are not just passive overseers; they are active participants in cultivating sustainability, fostering innovation, and ensuring ethical operations. However, finding the right individuals to fill these roles can be a challenge. What qualities should you look for in a board member? How can you attract people who are not only skilled but also deeply committed to your cause?

This chapter explores the foundational elements of building a successful board of directors. We will delve into the essential roles and responsibilities that define an effective board, outline the recruitment process for assembling a team with diverse expertise, and discuss best practices for onboarding new members. To support your journey, we also provide templates and practical tools to help you establish clear expectations and maintain a board that remains engaged, proactive, and aligned with your nonprofit's mission.

Roles, Responsibilities, and Legal Obligations

Every board member plays a vital role in the overall success of a nonprofit organization, serving as both a guiding force and a steadfast advocate for the mission. The role of a board member extends far beyond simply attending meetings; it is about setting the vision, ensuring sustainability, and fostering a culture of accountability and ethical leadership. Each decision made at the board level has a profound impact on the direction and effectiveness of the organization.

As a founder, it is essential to grasp the weight of these responsibilities, not only to build a strong board but also to nurture an environment where collaboration and strategic thinking thrive. A well-functioning board is one that not only governs but actively supports the nonprofit's initiatives, leveraging its collective expertise to navigate challenges and seize opportunities. When carefully curated, a board has the power to drive an organization forward, ensuring it remains mission-driven, financially sound, and adaptable in an ever-evolving landscape.

Key Roles of Board Members

An effective board is the heartbeat of a nonprofit, providing not just leadership, guidance, and accountability but also serving as the strategic compass that directs the organization toward its goals. While each member's specific contributions may differ based on their expertise, background, and level of engagement, they collectively ensure the organization remains financially sound, ethically responsible, and mission-driven. Board members are not just figureheads; they are dedicated stewards who use their skills, networks, and decision-making power to propel the nonprofit forward, weathering challenges and seizing opportunities that arise along the way. A strong board cultivates resilience, sustainability, and long-term success. Below are the key roles board members typically play:

- **Governance and Oversight**: At the heart of a nonprofit's success is its ability to stay true to its mission while evolving to meet the ever-changing needs of the community it serves. The board plays a pivotal role in ensuring that the organization's vision remains clear, its mission stays relevant, and its strategic direction is both ambitious and achievable. This responsibility requires board members to actively engage in high-level decision-making, continuously evaluate the nonprofit's impact, and anticipate future challenges. Through thoughtful governance, they provide a steady hand to guide the organization forward, ensuring that its values remain at the forefront of every initiative and that it is well-positioned to create meaningful and lasting change.

- **Fiduciary Responsibilities**: The financial health and sustainability of a nonprofit rest in the hands of its board, making fiduciary oversight one of the most critical responsibilities of board members. This role goes beyond simply approving budgets and reviewing financial statements—it requires a proactive commitment to ensuring that the organization remains financially sound, ethically responsible, and transparent in all fiscal matters. Board members must oversee audits, assess financial risks, and establish strong internal controls to prevent mismanagement or fraud. They must also ensure compliance with tax regulations and reporting requirements to maintain the organization's good standing. Ultimately, their vigilance and strategic decision-making in financial matters safeguard the nonprofit's long-term viability, allowing it to continue fulfilling its mission effectively.

- **Policy Setting**: One of the most vital responsibilities of a nonprofit board is to establish, review, and refine the policies that govern the organization's operations. Policies serve as the blueprint for decision-making, ensuring that the nonprofit remains aligned with its mission, maintains legal compliance, and upholds best practices in governance. Setting policies is not just about establishing rules; it is about creating a structured environment where the organization can thrive, grow, and adapt to changing circumstances. Board members must take a proactive role in reviewing existing policies, identifying gaps, and ensuring that all policies support the nonprofit's long-term vision. By doing so, they provide a clear framework that empowers staff, volunteers, and stakeholders to work cohesively toward the organization's goals while safeguarding its integrity and sustainability.

- **Advocacy and Public Relations**: Board members serve as the nonprofit's most dedicated champions, using their influence, networks, and voices to amplify the organization's mission and reach. Their advocacy extends beyond formal events and fundraisers; it happens in conversations with colleagues, in community gatherings, and even in casual interactions where they share the nonprofit's impact. Effective board members actively seek out opportunities to connect with potential donors, partners, and volunteers, reinforcing the nonprofit's credibility and expanding its support base. Whether engaging with policymakers, speaking at conferences, or leveraging media channels to raise awareness, their role in public relations is vital in fostering trust and elevating the organization's presence in the community.

- **Executive Director/CEO Support**: One of the most critical responsibilities of the board is selecting and supporting the executive director or CEO, the individual responsible for leading the nonprofit's day-to-day operations. This relationship is a partnership built on trust, communication, and shared commitment to the organization's mission. Hiring the right executive is just the beginning—

board members must also provide guidance, encouragement, and resources to ensure the leader thrives in their role. Regular evaluations and constructive feedback help the executive stay aligned with strategic goals while allowing for professional growth and course corrections when necessary. A well-supported executive director or CEO is more likely to lead effectively, fostering an organization that remains resilient, mission-driven, and impactful.

Responsibilities of Individual Board Members

Each board member plays an essential role in shaping the success of a nonprofit, and with that comes a set of personal responsibilities that extend beyond attending meetings. Being a board member is a commitment that requires active participation, strategic thinking, and a willingness to contribute time, expertise, and resources to the organization's mission. These responsibilities include:

- **Attendance**: Board meetings are more than just formalities; they are the strategic nerve center where key decisions are made, challenges are tackled, and the future of the nonprofit is shaped. A committed board member understands the significance of showing up—not just physically but mentally and emotionally. Active participation in discussions, committee work, and decision-making is essential to ensuring that the nonprofit stays on track toward fulfilling its mission. Regular attendance allows board members to remain informed, contribute meaningfully, and foster strong working relationships with fellow board members and leadership. By prioritizing attendance, board members demonstrate their dedication to the organization's success and play a direct role in driving its impact forward.

- **Financial Contributions**: A thriving nonprofit relies not only on external funding sources but also on the dedication of its leadership. Making a personal financial contribution is more than a monetary transaction—it is a declaration of commitment to the organization's mission. When board members personally invest in the nonprofit, they set a powerful example for donors, grantmakers, and the broader community. This contribution, whether large or small, signals confidence in the organization's work and fosters a culture of shared responsibility. It demonstrates that board members are not just advising from the sidelines but are actively invested in ensuring the nonprofit's success and sustainability.

- **Advocacy**: A board member's role extends far beyond meetings and decision-making—it involves being a vocal and passionate champion for the nonprofit's mission. Effective advocacy happens in both formal and informal settings, whether through networking events, personal conversations, or professional engagements. Board members are often the most trusted ambassadors of the organization, leveraging their influence and credibility to spread awareness, attract supporters, and inspire action. Their ability to tell the nonprofit's story compellingly and authentically plays a crucial role in building relationships with donors, partners, and the broader community. By embracing advocacy, board members contribute not only to the visibility of the nonprofit but also to its long-term growth and impact.

- **Skill Sharing**: Board members bring a wealth of professional expertise that can be instrumental in strengthening the nonprofit's operations and impact. Whether offering legal guidance, financial insights, HR strategies, marketing expertise, or technical knowledge, their contributions go beyond governance and directly enhance the organization's capacity to achieve its mission. By leveraging their skills, board members can mentor staff, streamline operations, and introduce innovative solutions to challenges. This engagement not only adds value to the nonprofit but also fosters a culture of collaboration, where board members feel more deeply connected to the cause they serve.

- **Legal Compliance**: A nonprofit operates within a complex framework of federal, state, and local regulations, and ensuring adherence to these laws is one of the board's most critical responsibilities. Legal compliance is not just about avoiding penalties—it is about upholding the integrity and credibility of the organization. Board members must stay informed about changes in nonprofit law, tax-exempt regulations, and reporting requirements to maintain the organization's good standing. From filing annual reports and ensuring charitable solicitation compliance to maintaining ethical governance practices, the board must provide oversight to prevent legal missteps. By fostering a culture of compliance, the board safeguards the nonprofit's mission, protects its assets, and strengthens public trust, ensuring that it remains a reputable and effective force for good.

Legal Obligations of the Board

Beyond their leadership roles and strategic responsibilities, board members carry a significant legal burden that underscores their accountability for the organization's actions and decisions. These legal obligations, known as fiduciary duties, are the foundation of ethical and responsible governance. Board members are not only stewards of the nonprofit's mission but also protectors of its financial health and legal standing. Their commitment to these obligations ensures transparency, trust, and long-term stability for the organization. These fiduciary duties include:

- **Duty of Care**: Board members have a profound responsibility to approach their role with diligence, thoughtfulness, and a deep commitment to the organization's success. Acting with the same level of care as a prudent individual in a similar leadership position means staying well-informed about the nonprofit's mission, financial health, and operational challenges. It involves actively engaging in board discussions, asking critical

65

questions, and making well-reasoned decisions based on accurate and up-to-date information. Board members must seek to understand the risks and opportunities facing the nonprofit, ensuring that their choices align with the long-term sustainability and impact of the organization. By demonstrating a commitment to careful oversight and strategic thinking, board members help foster an environment of accountability and responsible governance.

- **Duty of Loyalty**: Board members are entrusted with the nonprofit's mission and must consistently act in the organization's best interest, prioritizing its success over personal or external influences. This means exercising sound judgment, maintaining transparency, and avoiding conflicts of interest that could compromise decision-making. Whether it involves financial matters, strategic partnerships, or policy advocacy, board members must always place the organization's needs first. They should disclose any potential conflicts and recuse themselves from decisions where impartiality might be questioned. By upholding this duty, board members reinforce public trust, safeguard the nonprofit's integrity, and ensure that all actions align with the organization's core mission and values.

- **Duty of Obedience**: Board members hold a fundamental responsibility to ensure that the nonprofit remains steadfast in its mission, adheres to its governing bylaws, and complies with all relevant legal requirements. This duty is not just about following the rules—it is about safeguarding the integrity of the organization and ensuring that every decision aligns with its core purpose. Board members must remain vigilant in upholding the nonprofit's stated objectives, preventing mission drift, and ensuring that the organization's resources are used in a manner that advances its cause. This requires a deep understanding of the nonprofit's founding principles, continuous oversight of its programs and strategies, and a commitment to ethical leadership. By embracing the duty of obedience, board members reinforce the trust of donors, stakeholders, and the communities they serve, ensuring the organization remains a credible and impactful force for good.

Recruiting Board Members

Recruiting the right board members is a strategic and intentional process that goes beyond simply filling seats around a table. It's about assembling a group of individuals who bring wisdom, experience, and passion—trusted advisors who will help steer the organization toward long-term success. A well-rounded board is more than a collection of names; it is a team of dedicated leaders who lend their expertise, time, and influence to ensure the nonprofit remains mission-driven, financially stable, and poised for growth. The ideal board is diverse in skills, backgrounds, and perspectives, creating a dynamic environment where thoughtful decisions and innovative solutions can emerge. Finding the right people requires careful consideration, outreach, and a commitment to securing individuals who share the vision and are ready to actively contribute to its realization.

Essential Skills and Expertise

A well-rounded board is not just a collection of individuals but a dynamic team with a diverse mix of skills, backgrounds, and experiences. The strength of a nonprofit's board lies in its ability to bring together people who can offer valuable insights, strategic guidance, and practical expertise. A successful board is made up of individuals who complement each other's strengths and bring a variety of perspectives to the table. The right combination of skills helps the organization navigate challenges, seize opportunities, and drive meaningful change. Below are some of the essential areas of expertise to look for when building a well-balanced and effective board:

- **Legal Expertise**: Attorneys play a crucial role in ensuring that a nonprofit operates within the bounds of the law, safeguarding its tax-exempt status and protecting it from legal risks. They help navigate complex legal requirements, from drafting governance policies and reviewing contracts to advising on employment law and regulatory compliance. A skilled legal expert on the board can be instrumental in identifying potential liabilities before they become problems, ensuring that the nonprofit remains legally sound and ethically responsible. Their insights provide the organization with stability and confidence, allowing it to focus on fulfilling its mission without legal uncertainties looming in the background.

- **Financial Expertise**: Strong financial leadership is essential for the long-term sustainability of any nonprofit. Board members with backgrounds as CPAs, CFOs, or financial professionals bring invaluable expertise in managing budgets, overseeing audits, and ensuring responsible cash flow management. They help the organization maintain financial transparency, ensuring that donor funds and grant monies are allocated effectively and ethically. These financial stewards play a crucial role in risk management, identifying potential financial challenges before they escalate, and advising on sustainable strategies to enhance the organization's fiscal health. Their guidance allows the nonprofit to make informed decisions that support both short-term programmatic needs and long-term financial stability, ensuring the mission continues to thrive.

- **Fundraising Experience**: A nonprofit's financial sustainability often hinges on its ability to secure funding through diverse revenue streams, making board members with fundraising expertise invaluable assets. These individuals bring a deep understanding of donor cultivation, grant writing, and major gift campaigns, helping the organization build strong relationships with philanthropists, corporate sponsors, and foundation partners. Their experience allows them to identify opportunities for financial growth, create compelling fundraising strategies, and engage potential donors with persuasive storytelling. By leveraging their networks and expertise, they play a crucial role in ensuring that the nonprofit has the necessary resources to expand its programs, innovate solutions, and achieve long-term impact.

- **Human Resources/People Management**: The strength of any nonprofit lies in its people, and board members with expertise in human resources and people management play a crucial role in ensuring that the organization fosters a healthy, inclusive, and productive work environment. These individuals bring their knowledge of recruitment strategies, employee engagement, and conflict resolution to help shape policies that support staff and volunteers. They assist in onboarding new team members, advising on best practices for building a strong organizational culture, and navigating complex personnel challenges. By leveraging their HR expertise, they ensure that the nonprofit attracts and retains top talent, maintains fair and ethical employment practices, and cultivates a team dynamic that aligns with the mission and values of the organization.

- **Marketing and Communications**: The success of a nonprofit depends not only on the quality of its programs but also on how effectively it tells its story. Board members with expertise in marketing and communications help craft compelling narratives that connect with donors, stakeholders, and the broader community. They develop strategies to enhance brand visibility, ensuring that the nonprofit's mission and impact are consistently and persuasively communicated across various platforms. From social media campaigns and press outreach to donor engagement and thought leadership, their insights drive awareness and support. By leveraging their skills, they help the organization build a strong, trusted reputation, ultimately fostering deeper engagement and sustainable growth.

- **Industry-Specific Knowledge**: Every nonprofit operates within a unique landscape, facing challenges and opportunities specific to its sector. Board members with industry-specific expertise provide invaluable insights, ensuring that the organization stays ahead of trends, regulatory changes, and best practices relevant to its field. Whether working in healthcare, education, social justice, environmental advocacy, or another area, these subject-matter experts help bridge the gap between strategic vision and real-world execution. Their knowledge allows the nonprofit to make informed decisions, build credibility with funders and stakeholders, and remain competitive in an evolving landscape. By offering guidance on policy shifts, program development, and community engagement, they play a pivotal role in driving the organization's impact and long-term sustainability..

Recruitment Tips

Finding the right individuals to serve on your board can feel like an overwhelming task, but with a strategic approach, it becomes an opportunity to build a team that will elevate your nonprofit's mission. The key is to look beyond simply filling vacant seats and instead focus on identifying passionate, skilled, and committed individuals who can contribute meaningfully. A well-rounded board strengthens an organization, providing guidance, oversight, and expertise that are essential for long-term success. If you're wondering how to begin this process, the following strategies can provide a strong starting point:

- **Create a Board Matrix**: A well-structured board brings together individuals with a range of skills, perspectives, and lived experiences. To build a strong and effective team, it's essential to take stock of the expertise your board already has and identify gaps that need to be filled. A board matrix serves as a strategic tool to visualize where strengths lie and where there is room for improvement. By assessing the current board composition, you can determine which skills— such as financial acumen, legal expertise, fundraising experience, or community connections—are underrepresented. This proactive approach ensures that new board members are recruited with intention, creating a balanced and dynamic leadership team that can effectively guide the organization toward its mission-driven goals.

- **Use Networks**: Building a strong board begins with leveraging the connections you already have. Current board members, donors, and key stakeholders can be invaluable resources for identifying potential candidates who share a passion for your mission. These individuals often have professional networks filled with accomplished and dedicated leaders who may be eager to lend their expertise to a cause they care about. By tapping into these existing relationships, you can find individuals who not only bring the necessary skills but also align with the values and vision of your organization. Encouraging personal referrals also fosters a sense of trust and engagement, as prospective board members are more likely to be invested in a cause that comes recommended by someone they respect.

- **Advertise the Role**: Expanding the search beyond personal networks is crucial to attracting a diverse and qualified pool of candidates. Utilize nonprofit job boards, LinkedIn, and your organization's website to reach individuals who are actively looking for ways to contribute their expertise to meaningful causes. Craft a compelling and detailed board member posting that outlines the nonprofit's mission, the responsibilities of board service, and the skills or experiences most needed. Highlighting the impact a board member can have on the organization can help inspire passionate, mission-driven individuals to step forward and express interest. Additionally, consider promoting board openings through industry newsletters, professional associations, and local business groups to widen your reach and bring fresh perspectives to your leadership team.

- **Diversify Your Board**: A strong and effective board reflects the richness of the communities it serves. Striving for diversity in race, gender, age, socioeconomic background, and lived experiences ensures a breadth of perspectives that enhance decision-making, foster innovation, and strengthen the nonprofit's ability to meet the needs of diverse populations. A diverse board brings fresh insights, challenges assumptions, and broadens the organization's reach by connecting with communities that might otherwise be overlooked. By prioritizing inclusion, you cultivate a boardroom where different voices are valued, and collective wisdom leads to more impactful and equitable outcomes.

- **Conduct Informational Interviews**: Engaging in meaningful conversations with potential board members is a critical step in ensuring they align with your nonprofit's mission, values, and organizational culture. These interviews provide an opportunity to gauge their level of commitment, assess how their skills and expertise can benefit the board, and determine if their vision aligns with the strategic goals of the organization. Beyond qualifications, it's essential to evaluate their enthusiasm, willingness to contribute, and ability to collaborate with other board members. By fostering open and candid discussions, you can establish a strong foundation for a productive and engaged board that is truly invested in advancing the nonprofit's mission.

Board Agreements and Onboarding

Recruitment doesn't end when a board member agrees to join. In fact, that is just the beginning of their journey with the organization. A thoughtful and structured onboarding process is essential to ensure that new board members feel welcomed, informed, and empowered to contribute effectively. This process goes beyond simply handing them a packet of documents—it involves fostering a deep understanding of their role, clarifying expectations, and equipping them with the knowledge and resources needed to navigate their responsibilities with confidence. An engaging onboarding experience builds enthusiasm, strengthens commitment, and sets the stage for active participation, ultimately helping board members integrate seamlessly and make meaningful contributions to the organization's mission.

Board Agreement Template

Establishing clear expectations is essential for a successful board experience, and a board member agreement is a vital tool in achieving this clarity. This document is more than just a formality; it is a mutual commitment that outlines the responsibilities, expectations, and shared dedication between the board member and the nonprofit. By setting clear guidelines from the outset, the agreement fosters accountability, ensures alignment with the organization's mission, and reinforces a culture of trust and collaboration. It serves as a guiding framework, helping board members understand their role and the impact they can make while providing the organization with a structured approach to governance and engagement.

Sample Nonprofit Board Member Agreement

Purpose: This document outlines the roles, responsibilities, and commitments of [Name of Board Member] as a member of the Board of Directors for [Name of Nonprofit].

Term: The board member's term begins on [Start Date] and ends on [End Date].

Responsibilities:

1. Attend and actively participate in [X] board meetings annually.

2. Serve on at least one committee or working group.

3. Make a personal financial contribution of at least [$X] annually.

4. Serve as an advocate for [Name of Nonprofit] in the community.

5. Participate in an annual performance review of the Executive Director/CEO.

6. Follow the organization's conflict of interest and confidentiality policies.

Commitment: I, [Board Member Name], commit to fulfilling the responsibilities outlined in this agreement to the best of my ability. If I am unable to meet these obligations, I will notify the Board Chair.

Signatures: Board   Member   Signature:
_____

Date: _____

Board   Chair   Signature: _____
Date: _____

Sample Job Description for a Board Member

Setting clear expectations is crucial for new board members. This sample job description outlines the specific duties and responsibilities.

Title: Nonprofit   Board   Member
Reports   To: Board   Chair
Term: [X] years (renewable or non-renewable based on bylaws)

Primary Responsibilities:

- Attend and actively participate in [X] board meetings per year.

- Participate in one or more committees (e.g., finance, governance, development).

- Review and approve the annual budget, audit reports, and strategic plans.

- Provide oversight of the organization's mission, strategy, and goals.

- Ensure compliance with legal and ethical standards.

- Contribute to the organization's financial well-being through fundraising and personal giving.

- Advocate for the organization's mission in personal and professional networks.

Required Skills and Qualifications:

- Passion for the mission of [Name of Nonprofit].

- Ability to commit approximately [X] hours per month to board activities.

- Expertise in [legal, financial, fundraising, industry knowledge, etc.].

- Demonstrated experience in leadership, governance, or nonprofit management.

Preferred Skills:

- Prior board or committee experience.

- Knowledge of nonprofit financial statements.

Term: Board members serve a term of [X] years with the possibility of renewal [as specified by the bylaws].

Conclusion

Building a successful board of directors is not merely about assembling a group of individuals—it is about cultivating a dedicated team that will guide, support, and strengthen the nonprofit in meaningful ways. Thoughtful planning, strategic recruitment, and effective onboarding lay the groundwork for a board that is not only legally compliant but also deeply engaged in the organization's success. Clearly defining roles and responsibilities ensures that every member understands their contribution to governance and leadership, while a well-rounded mix of diverse skills and perspectives fosters robust decision-making and innovation.

For those looking to dive deeper into board governance best practices, *Effective Nonprofit Board Governance* offers invaluable insights on creating a high-functioning board, navigating complex challenges, and maximizing board member engagement. Drawing from real-world examples and expert guidance, this resource serves as an essential guide for building a board that not only fulfills its fiduciary duties but also acts as a strategic partner in advancing the organization's mission.

Once the right individuals are in place, a structured onboarding process solidifies their understanding of expectations and responsibilities, equipping them to serve as proactive stewards of the nonprofit's mission. With these essential elements in place, the board becomes a driving force, ensuring sustainability, accountability, and lasting impact in the community.

Operational Infrastructure: Setting Up Systems

Setting up the operational infrastructure of a nonprofit is akin to laying the foundation for a house—it's what holds everything together. Without a sturdy framework, even the most passionate mission can struggle under the weight of disorganization and inefficiency. A well-structured infrastructure provides the necessary support for programs to run seamlessly, for staff to work in alignment, and for organizational goals to be met with precision and clarity. When done right, it creates an adaptable system that fosters long-term sustainability and growth.

Think of governance as the blueprint—the carefully drawn plans that determine the structure and function of the organization. Who is responsible for making key decisions? Who oversees daily operations? The governance framework defines the roles of the board of directors, executive leadership, and key staff, ensuring that every individual knows their responsibilities and is empowered to fulfill them effectively. With a clear structure in place, the next step is establishing internal controls to protect against fraud, mismanagement, and inefficiencies. This involves implementing checks and balances, ensuring financial transparency, and adhering to best practices that promote ethical decision-making and accountability.

However, an organization is more than just a set of rules and controls—it requires systems that support efficiency, organization, and accessibility. A well-managed document storage system is essential for keeping vital records safe, while cloud-based platforms like Google Drive or Dropbox allow teams to collaborate and share files securely. Establishing an operational calendar that tracks grant deadlines, board meetings, compliance filings, and key events prevents important tasks from falling through the cracks. Furthermore, integrating performance metrics and evaluation tools ensures that your nonprofit stays on track and continuously improves, assessing its impact in real, measurable ways.

By putting these foundational elements in place, a nonprofit sets itself up for resilience, agility, and long-term impact. The right operational infrastructure is not just about avoiding chaos—it's about building a strong, dynamic organization that can grow, evolve, and thrive in pursuit of its mission.

Essential Policies and Procedures

If operational infrastructure is the foundation, then policies and procedures are the rules that govern how everything functions within an organization. Just as a well-run household depends on clear expectations and guidelines, a nonprofit thrives when everyone understands the standards for behavior, risk mitigation, and operational consistency. These guiding documents are not mere formalities; they establish fairness, protect the integrity of the mission, and ensure legal compliance at every level.

Start with governance policies, which define ethical decision-making and accountability. Every nonprofit should have a **Conflict of Interest Policy**, ensuring board members and staff act in the best interest of the organization, avoiding any personal gain at the expense of the mission. A **Whistleblower Policy** safeguards those who speak out against misconduct, fostering a culture of transparency and integrity. Additionally, a **Document Retention Policy** outlines how long critical records must be kept and when they can be securely disposed of, ensuring compliance with legal and regulatory requirements.

Operational policies play a crucial role in the day-to-day effectiveness of a nonprofit. These policies set the expectations for employee conduct, guide the responsible use of technology, and provide a framework for financial accountability. **Financial policies** establish clear protocols for managing resources, tracking expenditures, and ensuring fiscal responsibility. Procurement procedures help standardize purchasing, while reimbursement guidelines ensure expenses are handled consistently. Additionally, savings strategies clarify how funds should be allocated to build long-term financial health.

Human resources policies serve as a backbone for fair and equitable treatment of employees and volunteers. A well-crafted **Employee Handbook** details workplace expectations, benefits, and conduct standards. **Equal Employment Opportunity (EEO) statements** reaffirm the nonprofit's commitment to diversity and inclusion. Training policies, performance evaluations, and dispute resolution mechanisms ensure that staff members are supported in their professional development and that issues are addressed constructively.

Finally, programmatic policies guide how services are delivered, ensuring consistency, ethical practice, and measurable impact. These policies define how client information is protected, how program effectiveness is assessed, and how compliance with grant requirements is maintained. As a nonprofit evolves, its policies must be reviewed and updated regularly to remain relevant and aligned with best practices.

By establishing and adhering to comprehensive policies and procedures, a nonprofit ensures that its mission is carried out with integrity, efficiency, and resilience. As outlined in *Policies and Procedures for Nonprofit Success*, part of the *Nonprofit Success Toolkit Series*, having clear and well-documented policies is essential not only for compliance but also for fostering a culture of accountability and operational excellence. This book provides a step-by-step guide for developing key policies in governance, finance, human resources, and program operations, helping organizations establish a strong foundation from day one.

These guidelines serve as a strategic roadmap for decision-making, helping organizations proactively manage challenges, mitigate risks, and maintain operational excellence. By implementing best practices and regularly updating policies to reflect changing needs, nonprofits can ensure they remain adaptable, transparent, and mission-driven.

For organizations looking to get started, MBS Operational Services offers free policy and procedure templates that can be accessed at MBS Free Resources:

https://mbsoperations.com/free-resources. These templates provide a practical starting point for crafting policies that align with your nonprofit's mission and operational needs. By utilizing these tools and the guidance provided in *Policies and Procedures for Nonprofit Success*, nonprofits can build the trust of stakeholders, donors, and the communities they serve while laying a solid foundation for sustainable growth.

Technology Tools for Startups

Nonprofits often operate on limited budgets, making it tempting to delay investments in technology. However, leveraging the right tools from the start can streamline operations, reduce administrative burdens, and ultimately save both time and money. By strategically incorporating essential technology, nonprofits can enhance efficiency, improve communication, and strengthen donor relationships—critical elements for long-term sustainability.

Every nonprofit should consider essential tools across six key categories. These tools help ensure smooth day-to-day operations, allowing teams to focus more on mission-driven work rather than administrative complexities. Without them, organizations risk inefficiencies that can drain valuable resources and hinder impact. From financial management to donor engagement, having the right technology in place is not an option—it's a necessity for growth and success in today's digital landscape.

Accounting Software is a fundamental necessity for nonprofits, not just a convenience. Managing financial health with accuracy and transparency is critical for sustaining operations, maintaining donor trust, and complying with grant requirements. Tools like QuickBooks and Xero simplify financial tracking, making it easier to monitor revenue, manage expenses, and ensure that restricted and unrestricted funds are properly accounted for. These platforms allow nonprofits to generate essential reports that demonstrate financial accountability to boards, funders, and regulatory bodies.

Beyond accounting, nonprofits must also prioritize donor relationships, as they are the lifeblood of the organization's funding base. A **Customer Relationship Management (CRM) system** like Salesforce or Bloomerang is essential for tracking donor contributions, managing donor interactions, and analyzing fundraising efforts. These platforms help organizations build stronger relationships by personalizing engagement, segmenting donor data for targeted outreach, and automating follow-ups. A well-maintained CRM ensures that every donor feels valued and connected to the mission, fostering long-term support and sustainable funding streams.

By integrating robust accounting software and a reliable CRM, nonprofits can create a seamless financial and donor management system that enhances organizational efficiency, reduces errors, and positions them for future growth.

Project Management Software plays a vital role in ensuring that nonprofit teams remain aligned, organized, and efficient. In a world where remote collaboration and multi-tasking are the norm, tools like Asana and Trello help structure workflows, assign responsibilities, and track progress in a clear, visually engaging way. These platforms allow teams to break down projects into manageable tasks, set deadlines, and provide real-time updates, ensuring that nothing falls through the cracks.

For a deeper dive into the best project management tools for nonprofits, refer to *The Nonprofit Project Management Handbook*, part of the *Nonprofit Success Toolkit Series*. In Chapter 5, I break down the strengths and weaknesses of platforms like Asana, Trello, Monday.com, and ClickUp, outlining how each can be leveraged for different types of nonprofit projects. Whether working on grant proposals, organizing events, or managing volunteer programs, selecting the right project management tool can significantly increase accountability and streamline processes across the organization.

Meanwhile, **File Sharing and Document Management** solutions are indispensable for modern nonprofits. Cloud-based storage options like Google Drive and Dropbox provide secure, easy access to essential documents from anywhere, eliminating the risk of lost paperwork and reducing dependence on physical storage. These tools allow teams to collaborate on files in real time, track revisions, and ensure that up-to-date versions of critical documents, such as grant applications, policy handbooks, and donor records, are always accessible. Having a reliable document management system in place fosters better organization, security, and efficiency, ultimately supporting a more productive and connected team.

Don't overlook **Communication Tools**, as they are the lifeblood of internal coordination and external engagement. Nonprofits rely on clear and effective communication to keep teams connected, engage supporters, and amplify their mission. Email marketing platforms like **Mailchimp** allow organizations to create visually appealing campaigns that keep donors, volunteers, and stakeholders informed about impact stories, fundraising initiatives, and upcoming events. Additionally, internal communication tools like **Slack** or **Microsoft Teams** ensure seamless collaboration among staff and volunteers, helping to bridge geographical gaps and maintain real-time coordination.

Beyond communication, **Fundraising Platforms** are essential in today's digital landscape, providing nonprofits with the means to cultivate donor relationships and generate revenue. Platforms like **Classy** and **Givebutter** enable organizations to create compelling donation pages, launch peer-to-peer fundraising campaigns, and track donor engagement metrics. These tools streamline the giving process, making it easier for supporters to contribute and stay involved. As highlighted in *The Nonprofit Project Management Handbook*, selecting the right communication and fundraising tools is crucial for long-term sustainability and operational efficiency. Chapter 7 of the book delves into how nonprofits can optimize these platforms for maximum impact, helping organizations grow their outreach and fundraising efforts in a scalable way.

Prioritize tools that grow with your organization, ensuring that as your nonprofit expands, your communication and fundraising strategies evolve alongside it.

Banking, Accounting, and Bookkeeping

Effective financial management is crucial from the very first day a nonprofit begins operating. It's not just about keeping track of money—it's about fostering a culture of accountability, transparency, and trust that extends to donors, board members, and the communities you serve. The financial systems you establish early on will lay the groundwork for long-term sustainability and credibility, ensuring that your organization is not only compliant but also strategically positioned for growth.

Start with banking—the backbone of financial infrastructure. Open a dedicated bank account specifically for the nonprofit, separate from personal or business accounts, to ensure clear financial boundaries. Seek out banking institutions that understand nonprofit needs and offer reduced fees, grant-friendly features, or specialized services that cater to mission-driven organizations. Establishing this financial separation not only simplifies accounting but also builds credibility when dealing with funders and auditors.

Once banking is in place, the next step is setting up a **robust accounting system**. Investing in accounting software like QuickBooks or Xero allows nonprofits to track income, expenses, and grants efficiently, while also generating financial reports that provide clear insights into organizational health. One key practice is to ensure that your **chart of accounts** is structured to distinguish between program revenue, restricted funds, and grant income. This level of detail is crucial when reporting to funders and maintaining compliance with grant agreements.

Bookkeeping Best Practices can make or break a nonprofit's financial health. Monthly reconciliation of bank statements prevents discrepancies from becoming larger issues down the road. It's also essential to track **restricted versus unrestricted funds** separately—this ensures that donor contributions designated for specific projects are used appropriately and do not get inadvertently absorbed into general expenses. Using payroll services to accurately process employee wages and tax withholdings adds another layer of financial stability. To further minimize financial risk, establish **internal controls** by assigning different individuals to handle various financial responsibilities—such as one person processing payments and another reconciling accounts. Regular internal audits will help detect potential issues before they escalate and provide peace of mind to leadership and stakeholders.

When it's time to apply for grants, your financial records will be one of your strongest assets. Funders want assurance that their contributions are being handled responsibly and making a tangible impact. Having a well-documented financial system, transparent reporting, and a commitment to sound bookkeeping practices will set your nonprofit apart as a responsible steward of donor funds, increasing your chances of securing funding and long-term support.

By establishing these financial best practices from the outset, nonprofits can lay a solid foundation for sustainability and success.

Compliance and Risk Management

Navigating the complex web of nonprofit compliance and risk management can feel overwhelming, but it is essential to maintaining your organization's integrity, financial health, and public trust. Government regulations at the federal, state, and local levels are constantly evolving, and nonprofits must stay vigilant to avoid penalties, loss of tax-exempt status, or reputational damage. The key to staying ahead is a proactive approach that embeds compliance and risk management into the fabric of daily operations.

One of the most fundamental aspects of compliance is understanding your **Annual Filings**. Each year, nonprofits must submit IRS Form 990, a public financial disclosure that ensures transparency and maintains tax-exempt status. Additionally, state-specific requirements may mandate annual registration for fundraising activities, sales tax exemptions, or charitable solicitation permits. Tracking these deadlines in an **operational compliance calendar** helps prevent last-minute scrambles and costly oversights.

Beyond paperwork, nonprofits must also be mindful of **Licenses and Permits**. Organizations that provide food services, host public events, or engage in specialized programming may require industry-specific permits to remain legally compliant. Conducting regular regulatory audits ensures that your organization meets all necessary legal requirements and avoids unexpected roadblocks.

However, compliance extends beyond government regulations—it also involves preparing for unforeseen risks that could disrupt operations. **Risk management** is not just about having the right documents in place; it's about ensuring your organization is resilient in the face of uncertainty. Securing **Insurance Coverage** is a critical step in protecting your nonprofit from potential liabilities. Policies such as general liability, **Directors & Officers (D&O) liability**, and workers' compensation safeguard the organization, its leaders, and employees from financial and legal consequences.

An essential component of risk management is having a **Crisis Management Plan**. Unexpected events—whether natural disasters, cybersecurity breaches, or public relations crises—can severely impact a nonprofit's operations and credibility. By developing and regularly updating an emergency preparedness plan, nonprofits can ensure they have clear communication protocols, response teams, and contingency strategies in place to mitigate disruption and maintain public trust.

Board leadership plays a crucial role in overseeing compliance and risk mitigation. Regular updates on **regulatory changes**, financial audits, and organizational risk assessments help board members stay informed and engaged in safeguarding the nonprofit's stability. Conducting **periodic risk evaluations** allows leadership to identify vulnerabilities and implement solutions before they escalate into larger problems.

At its core, compliance and risk management are not just about avoiding penalties; they are about safeguarding the nonprofit's mission and ensuring its ability to serve the community for years to come. A proactive, structured approach fosters credibility, strengthens donor confidence, and positions the organization for long-term success. When compliance and risk mitigation become integral parts of your nonprofit's operations, you are not just protecting the present—you are securing the future of your mission.

Human Resources (HR) Management

Building a nonprofit team requires careful planning, intentional hiring, and continuous support to ensure that employees and volunteers thrive within the organization. Recruiting the right individuals goes beyond simply filling positions—it involves finding people who are passionate about the mission and equipped with the skills needed to contribute meaningfully. A well-structured onboarding process helps new team members integrate smoothly, understand their roles, and feel connected to the organization's purpose from day one.

However, recruitment is just the beginning. Effective human resources management ensures that staff members feel valued, supported, and motivated to perform at their best. This includes establishing clear job descriptions, offering professional development opportunities, and creating an environment where open communication is encouraged. Regular performance evaluations, mentorship programs, and pathways for career advancement help retain dedicated employees and prevent burnout.

A strong HR strategy also involves prioritizing workplace culture and employee well-being. By fostering a supportive and inclusive environment, nonprofits can cultivate a team that is resilient, collaborative, and committed to driving meaningful change. Ultimately, investing in human resources management is not just about maintaining operations—it's about building an engaged and inspired workforce that will help the nonprofit achieve its long-term goals.

Start with **Recruitment and Hiring**, as the success of a nonprofit hinges on assembling a team that is both skilled and passionate about the mission. Begin by clearly defining job roles and responsibilities to ensure expectations are set from the outset. Develop a structured and thoughtful interview process that not only evaluates a candidate's qualifications but also assesses their alignment with the organization's values and culture. Incorporate behavioral and situational interview questions to gauge problem-solving abilities, teamwork, and adaptability—key qualities for thriving in a nonprofit environment.

Once a candidate is selected, a well-structured onboarding program is essential for setting them up for success. Effective onboarding goes beyond paperwork and orientation—it's about immersing new hires in the mission, introducing them to key stakeholders, and providing them with the resources needed to hit the ground running. Assigning a mentor or peer guide can further ease the transition, fostering a sense of belonging and immediate engagement with the team. Investing in a comprehensive hiring and onboarding strategy ensures that employees feel connected, motivated, and equipped to contribute meaningfully to the organization's goals.

Performance Management is an ongoing and dynamic process that fosters growth, accountability, and professional development within a nonprofit. It begins with setting clear, measurable goals that align with both the individual's role and the broader mission of the organization. These goals provide direction and motivation, ensuring that employees understand how their contributions impact the success of the nonprofit.

Providing regular feedback is essential in keeping staff engaged and improving performance over time. Feedback should be both constructive and encouraging, offering employees a roadmap for improvement while recognizing their successes. This can be done through informal check-ins, peer feedback, and structured review meetings.

A key element of performance management is offering development opportunities. Investing in professional growth—through workshops, mentorship programs, leadership training, and skill-building initiatives—ensures that employees feel valued and equipped to take on greater responsibilities within the organization. Career development plans, tailored to individual strengths and aspirations, can further enhance employee retention and engagement.

Formal **performance evaluations** play a vital role in assessing progress and identifying areas for growth. These evaluations should be structured yet flexible, incorporating self-assessments, peer reviews, and supervisor feedback to provide a well-rounded perspective on an employee's performance. By maintaining a culture of continuous improvement and open communication, nonprofits can build strong, motivated teams that drive the organization toward long-term success.

Employee Policies serve as the guiding principles that shape the work environment, ensuring fairness, accountability, and transparency within the organization. A well-structured **Employee Handbook** is more than just a document—it is a vital resource that communicates expectations, rights, and responsibilities to staff members. This handbook should include detailed policies on leave entitlements, health and retirement benefits, performance expectations, and professional conduct, ensuring that every employee understands their role within the organization and what is required of them.

Beyond just stating policies, organizations should actively engage employees in **training programs** that reinforce workplace values and create a culture of respect and inclusivity. Comprehensive training on harassment prevention and workplace safety not only fulfills legal requirements but also fosters an environment where employees feel safe, valued, and empowered. Regular workshops, open discussions, and accessible reporting mechanisms can further reinforce these principles, encouraging a proactive approach to maintaining a healthy work culture.

By implementing and consistently updating employee policies, nonprofits can create a work environment that supports productivity, well-being, and organizational success, ensuring that staff members remain motivated and aligned with the mission.

Ensuring compliance with **Labor Laws** and regulations is not just about legal obligations—it's about fostering a fair and equitable workplace where employees feel valued and protected. Nonprofits must stay up-to-date with wage and hour laws to guarantee fair compensation for staff and prevent costly violations. Workplace safety regulations help create a secure environment, reducing risks and liabilities while promoting the well-being of employees and volunteers.

Beyond basic compliance, organizations should proactively implement policies that reflect their commitment to equity and inclusion. **Anti-discrimination laws** serve as the foundation for fostering a diverse and inclusive workforce. By integrating diversity training, transparent hiring practices, and a culture of respect, nonprofits can go beyond mere legal adherence and create a truly welcoming environment for all employees.

To maintain compliance, it's essential to regularly review labor policies, stay informed about legislative changes, and provide ongoing training for leadership and staff. Establishing clear reporting mechanisms for grievances and conducting periodic audits can further reinforce a culture of fairness and accountability. By prioritizing labor law compliance, nonprofits protect their staff, enhance their reputation, and ensure long-term organizational sustainability.

Facilities Management

Managing your nonprofit's physical space is an essential part of operations, directly influencing not just safety and functionality, but also the overall experience of your team, volunteers, and community members. The environment in which a nonprofit operates plays a crucial role in its ability to fulfill its mission effectively. Whether your organization is housed in a small office, a co-working space, or a multi-use facility, every aspect of facilities management contributes to creating a workspace that fosters productivity, collaboration, and a sense of purpose.

Thoughtful planning begins with assessing the needs of the organization. Does your team require private offices, or is an open workspace more conducive to collaboration? Is there a need for community gathering spaces, storage for supplies, or dedicated areas for client services? These questions help shape how the space is utilized to optimize efficiency and accessibility.

Beyond day-to-day functionality, facilities management also involves maintaining a safe and secure environment. Proper upkeep of infrastructure, adherence to local building codes, and proactive maintenance schedules prevent costly repairs and disruptions. Investing in security measures—such as controlled access points, surveillance cameras, and emergency preparedness plans—ensures the safety of staff, visitors, and critical assets.

Additionally, cost efficiency is a key factor in facilities management. Nonprofits must carefully balance expenses, whether it's negotiating lease agreements, managing utility costs, or seeking in-kind donations for office furnishings and renovations. A well-maintained and thoughtfully designed workspace can enhance productivity, reduce operational inefficiencies, and create an atmosphere that reflects the organization's mission and values.

Ultimately, effective facilities management is about more than just maintaining a building—it's about curating an environment that supports and strengthens the work of the organization. By intentionally planning and managing physical space, nonprofits can create a welcoming, functional, and sustainable setting where their mission can thrive.

Start with **Facility Planning and Space Allocation**, as the way a nonprofit organizes its physical space can directly impact efficiency, collaboration, and the overall success of its mission. Before securing a space or making modifications, take the time to conduct a thorough assessment of the organization's needs. How many staff members require dedicated offices or workstations? Is there a need for communal spaces where teams can collaborate, or private areas for confidential meetings and counseling services? Storage requirements for equipment, supplies, or program materials should also be factored into the planning process to ensure resources are accessible yet neatly organized.

Beyond immediate operational needs, it's important to consider how shared spaces—such as conference rooms, event areas, or multipurpose facilities—will be utilized. Establishing clear usage policies and scheduling systems can help prevent conflicts and maximize the efficiency of these spaces. For example, creating a shared digital calendar for meeting rooms or designating specific zones for high-traffic activities can prevent bottlenecks and ensure smoother daily operations.

A well-planned facility layout fosters productivity and enhances the experience for staff, volunteers, and program participants alike. By carefully allocating space to balance functionality and flexibility, nonprofits can create an environment that not only supports their immediate work but also adapts to future growth and evolving community needs.

Lease Agreements are more than just paperwork—they represent a long-term commitment that can impact a nonprofit's financial stability and operational flexibility. When entering into a lease, it is essential to thoroughly understand the terms and conditions to ensure they align with your organization's needs and budget. Pay close attention to renewal clauses, escalation clauses for rent increases, and any hidden costs such as maintenance fees, utilities, and property management expenses. Additionally, consider whether the lease allows for subleasing or modifications to the space, as these factors could provide much-needed adaptability as your organization grows.

Engaging a legal professional to review the lease agreement before signing can prevent costly surprises and ensure that your nonprofit is adequately protected. A lawyer with experience in nonprofit real estate matters can help identify potential risks, negotiate more favorable terms, and clarify responsibilities related to maintenance and liability. Taking the time to carefully review and negotiate lease agreements not only safeguards your organization's financial health but also provides peace of mind, knowing that your physical space supports your mission without unnecessary constraints or unexpected expenses.

Maintenance and Repairs are the backbone of a safe, efficient, and welcoming nonprofit workspace. Keeping a facility in top condition requires more than just occasional fixes—it demands a proactive approach to identifying and addressing potential issues before they escalate into costly, disruptive problems. Regular inspections should be scheduled to assess the condition of key infrastructure elements, such as electrical systems, plumbing, HVAC units, and overall structural integrity. These evaluations help to detect early signs of wear and tear, allowing for timely interventions that prevent larger breakdowns.

Assigning a dedicated **facilities coordinator** ensures that there is always someone overseeing maintenance schedules, coordinating with vendors, and responding promptly to urgent repair needs. For organizations without an in-house facilities team, partnering with a **property management company** can provide expertise in handling repairs, overseeing long-term maintenance planning, and ensuring compliance with local building codes and safety standards.

Beyond scheduled upkeep, nonprofits should also establish a clear protocol for handling emergency repairs. Whether it's a burst pipe, electrical failure, or security breach, having a defined response plan—complete with contact lists for emergency contractors—helps minimize disruptions and keeps operations running smoothly. Investing in preventative maintenance is not just about fixing problems as they arise; it's about preserving the longevity of the workspace, ensuring a safe environment, and protecting the resources that allow the organization to thrive.

Safety and Security are fundamental pillars in ensuring the well-being of your staff, visitors, and the overall integrity of your nonprofit's operations. A safe and secure environment not only fosters productivity and peace of mind but also reinforces trust among stakeholders, donors, and community members who rely on your organization's services.

Start by assessing potential security risks within your facility. Consider installing **alarm systems, security cameras, and controlled access entry points** to safeguard against unauthorized access and theft. These measures provide real-time monitoring and deterrence, ensuring that sensitive information, valuable equipment, and individuals on-site remain protected. A security assessment conducted by professionals can help identify weak points and recommend solutions tailored to your nonprofit's specific needs.

Beyond physical security, it is crucial to develop an **emergency response and evacuation plan**. Unexpected events such as natural disasters, fire outbreaks, or security threats can disrupt operations and put lives at risk. Establishing **clear evacuation routes, emergency contact lists, and designated safety officers** ensures that everyone knows their role in a crisis. Regular **drills and training sessions** help staff and volunteers respond calmly and efficiently in emergency situations, reducing panic and potential harm.

Additionally, security extends beyond the physical realm to include **data protection and cybersecurity**. Nonprofits store sensitive donor information, financial records, and confidential client data, making them potential targets for cyber threats. Implementing **password protection policies, multi-factor authentication, and data encryption** can help prevent breaches and ensure compliance with privacy regulations.

By integrating comprehensive safety and security measures into your daily operations, your nonprofit not only minimizes risks but also demonstrates a commitment to the well-being of everyone involved. Prioritizing these strategies will help maintain a secure, resilient, and trusted organization that can focus on advancing its mission without unnecessary disruptions.

Insurance Coverage is a cornerstone of responsible nonprofit management, ensuring that your organization is protected from unexpected risks that could otherwise derail your mission. From natural disasters to legal liabilities, insurance acts as a safeguard, allowing nonprofits to focus on their work without constant fear of financial instability due to unforeseen events.

At a minimum, your nonprofit should have **general liability insurance**, which provides coverage for accidents, injuries, or property damage that may occur during operations. Additionally, **property insurance** is essential for organizations that own or lease physical space, protecting against damage from fires, floods, theft, and other disasters. If your nonprofit provides professional services or advice, **professional liability insurance** (sometimes called errors and omissions insurance) can protect against claims of negligence or inadequate service.

Beyond these basic coverages, consider **Directors and Officers (D&O) insurance**, which shields board members and executives from personal financial liability arising from decisions made on behalf of the organization. Workers' compensation insurance is also critical if your nonprofit has employees, ensuring protection for both the organization and staff in the event of work-related injuries.

Reviewing your policy annually is crucial, as a nonprofit's needs can shift due to growth, changes in services, or expansion into new areas. As your facility, assets, and operations evolve, it's important to adjust coverage to ensure comprehensive protection. Engaging an insurance professional who specializes in nonprofit policies can provide valuable insights into the specific risks your organization faces and the best coverage options available.

Ultimately, having the right insurance in place is about more than just meeting legal requirements—it's about securing the longevity of your nonprofit, instilling confidence in donors and stakeholders, and ensuring that your mission remains on track even in the face of unexpected challenges.

Ensuring the facility complies with **Accessibility Requirements** is not just a legal obligation—it's a commitment to inclusion and equity. Every nonprofit should strive to create a space where all individuals, regardless of ability, can fully participate in and benefit from its programs and services.

A truly accessible environment goes beyond merely meeting the basic standards outlined in the **Americans with Disabilities Act (ADA)**. It requires thoughtful planning to eliminate barriers and foster a welcoming atmosphere for people of all mobility levels, sensory needs, and cognitive abilities. This includes installing **ramps, elevators, and automatic doors** for those with mobility impairments, ensuring **clear signage with Braille** for visually impaired individuals, and designing **quiet spaces or sensory-friendly areas** for those with neurological conditions.

Moreover, accessibility should extend to digital spaces as well. Nonprofits should ensure their websites, communication materials, and virtual events are compatible with screen readers, provide captions for videos, and offer multiple ways for individuals to engage with their content. By integrating these thoughtful modifications, nonprofits can demonstrate their commitment to inclusivity and ensure that all stakeholders—regardless of ability—can fully engage with and contribute to the mission.

By prioritizing accessibility, nonprofits don't just comply with regulations—they create a space where dignity, respect, and equal opportunity are woven into the fabric of their work.

Effective facilities management isn't just about maintaining a building—it's about creating a safe, welcoming, and functional environment where your mission can thrive.

Conclusion

Building a nonprofit from the ground up is no small feat. It requires not only passion and vision but also the dedication to develop a strong operational infrastructure that can withstand the challenges of growth and sustainability. The foundation of a thriving nonprofit lies in establishing clear policies, leveraging the right technology, and managing finances, compliance, HR, and facilities with precision. Each of these components plays a crucial role in shaping an organization that is not only stable and efficient but also adaptable to the evolving needs of the communities it serves.

Building a Fundraising Plan

Where Nonprofits Get Their Money

To develop an effective fundraising strategy, it is crucial to first understand the financial landscape in which nonprofits operate. Unlike for-profit businesses, nonprofits rely on a variety of funding sources to sustain their missions and drive impact. Generally, nonprofit revenue comes from four primary streams: grants, donations, earned income, and fees for service. Each of these plays a unique role in shaping the organization's financial health and long-term sustainability.

Grants are a significant source of funding for many nonprofits, provided by foundations, government agencies, and corporations. These funds are often earmarked for specific projects or initiatives, meaning that recipients must go through a rigorous application process and meet stringent reporting requirements. While grants can offer large sums of money, they are also highly competitive and not always a guaranteed source of long-term support.

Donations represent another cornerstone of nonprofit funding. Individuals, families, and community groups contribute to causes they care about through one-time gifts or recurring donations. These gifts often come in response to online fundraising campaigns, direct mail solicitations, or major donor outreach efforts. Unlike grants, donations can provide more flexible funding, allowing nonprofits to cover operational costs and expand their initiatives as needed.

In addition to these traditional funding sources, earned income has become an increasingly important strategy for financial stability. Earned income refers to money generated through the sale of goods and services that align with the nonprofit's mission. This could include offering educational programs for a fee, selling branded merchandise, or charging for specialized training and consulting services. Many nonprofits develop earned income strategies to lessen their dependence on unpredictable funding streams, creating a self-sustaining revenue model that supports their long-term goals.

Fees for service operate in a similar fashion, as nonprofits charge for providing specific services to individuals or other organizations. This could include a community health clinic charging for medical appointments, a nonprofit consulting firm offering expertise to other charities, or an arts organization selling tickets to performances. By incorporating these fee-based models, nonprofits can generate a steady stream of revenue that supports their mission-driven work while simultaneously providing value to their stakeholders.

A well-balanced financial strategy combines these diverse revenue streams, ensuring that no single source dominates the organization's funding. By thoughtfully blending grants, donations, earned income, and fees for service, nonprofits can build resilience against financial uncertainties and continue making a meaningful impact in their communities.

Understanding Earned vs. Donated Income

Earned income and donated income represent two distinct financial lifelines for nonprofits, each offering unique advantages and playing a critical role in overall organizational stability. Donated income is the lifeblood of many nonprofits, coming from the generosity of individuals, foundations, and corporations. These funds, while often unrestricted and flexible, can sometimes be designated for specific initiatives or projects. The success of donated income largely hinges on the strength of fundraising appeals, donor stewardship, and the cultivation of long-term relationships with supporters.

On the other hand, earned income is derived from the sale of products, services, or programs that align with the nonprofit's mission. Unlike donations, which depend on the goodwill of external contributors, earned income is directly linked to an organization's ability to provide value through its offerings. Examples of earned income include fees for workshops, paid training programs, consulting services, and even the sale of mission-related products. By integrating earned income into their revenue strategy, nonprofits gain a degree of financial autonomy, reducing dependence on unpredictable donor funding cycles and ensuring a steady cash flow to sustain operations.

Balancing these two revenue streams allows nonprofits to maximize their impact while maintaining financial health. While donor relationships and grants offer essential support, developing an earned income strategy creates an additional layer of resilience, ensuring that the organization can thrive even in times of economic uncertainty.

Incorporating Earned Income Into Your Business Model

To successfully integrate earned income into a nonprofit's business model, organizations must take a strategic and mission-driven approach. This requires careful consideration of the organization's strengths, expertise, and potential revenue-generating opportunities. The first step is identifying services or products that naturally align with the nonprofit's mission and could provide value to the community in a way that generates revenue. For example, a nonprofit focused on education might monetize training programs, offer consulting services to other organizations, or develop and sell educational materials.

Once a viable earned income opportunity is identified, it is essential to conduct thorough market research. This involves understanding the needs and preferences of potential customers, evaluating competitor offerings, and determining appropriate pricing strategies. By identifying gaps in the market and differentiating their services, nonprofits can position themselves competitively while staying true to their mission. Additionally, organizations should develop a detailed business plan that outlines cost structures, revenue projections, and the operational requirements needed to sustain and grow the earned income initiative.

Implementation requires investment in the necessary infrastructure to ensure seamless service delivery. This might involve hiring staff with specialized skills, setting up customer support systems, or leveraging technology for e-commerce and digital transactions. Nonprofits should also prioritize marketing and outreach efforts to ensure visibility and attract potential customers. By leveraging social media, partnerships, and targeted advertising, organizations can effectively promote their earned income initiatives to the right audience.

Once launched, continuous evaluation is critical to ensuring long-term success. Organizations should establish metrics to track financial performance, customer satisfaction, and operational efficiency. Regular assessments allow for necessary adjustments to improve offerings, optimize pricing, and refine marketing strategies. By treating earned income initiatives with the same level of strategic planning and oversight as other funding sources, nonprofits can build sustainable revenue streams that complement donations and grants.

By thoughtfully integrating earned income into their financial model, nonprofits not only enhance their financial sustainability but also strengthen their ability to fulfill their mission. Diversifying revenue streams allows organizations to be more resilient in the face of funding fluctuations, ensuring long-term impact and stability.

By developing a comprehensive strategy that blends both earned and donated income, nonprofits can create a more resilient and adaptable financial foundation. Earned income provides a level of autonomy, allowing organizations to generate funds through services and products that align with their mission, while donated income offers the flexibility and support of generous contributors who believe in the cause. A well-balanced approach ensures that when one revenue stream faces challenges, another can help bridge the gap. This diversification mitigates financial instability, enabling nonprofits to focus on long-term growth, strategic initiatives, and expanding their impact without being overly dependent on any single funding source. By thoughtfully integrating both income streams, nonprofits not only secure their financial future but also strengthen their ability to fulfill their mission, even in times of economic uncertainty.

How to Write a Basic Fundraising Plan

Creating a fundraising plan for the first year is essential for ensuring financial sustainability and long-term success. This process begins with setting clear and achievable goals that align with your nonprofit's mission and operational needs. Start by determining the total revenue you aim to raise for the year, then break it down into manageable monthly or quarterly targets. Consider all potential revenue streams, including grants, individual donations, earned income, and service fees, to build a diversified funding approach that reduces reliance on any single source.

With goals in place, the next step is to outline key fundraising activities that will drive financial support. This could involve submitting grant proposals to funding organizations, launching targeted donor appeals through direct mail and digital campaigns, or hosting fundraising events. Each initiative should have a corresponding timeline and clear objectives to ensure that efforts remain focused and strategic. Additionally, audience segmentation plays a vital role in effective fundraising. By identifying and understanding the motivations of potential donors, grantors, and customers, your nonprofit can craft tailored outreach efforts that resonate with each group and encourage deeper engagement.

A comprehensive strategy should also include specific fundraising methods for each revenue stream. For grants, conduct thorough research to identify relevant opportunities and set a goal to apply for at least five viable funding sources. When seeking donations, consider launching a structured annual campaign, complete with storytelling elements and impact-driven messaging to inspire support. If your organization generates income through services, explore ways to enhance these offerings, such as introducing a paid membership program or expanding workshop offerings to generate additional revenue.

Budgeting is another essential aspect of the fundraising plan. Estimate the costs associated with your fundraising initiatives, including expenses for promotional materials, software, staff time, and event logistics. Identify the tools that will support your efforts, such as donor management platforms, email marketing software, and financial tracking systems, ensuring you have the necessary infrastructure to manage your fundraising efficiently.

Finally, tracking progress and evaluating success is critical to refining and improving future fundraising efforts. Establish key performance indicators (KPIs) such as donor retention rates, total funds raised, and return on investment (ROI). Regularly review these metrics to assess what's working well and where adjustments may be needed. By continuously monitoring and adapting your approach, your nonprofit can build a strong, sustainable fundraising foundation that supports its mission and long-term growth.

Grant-Writing Basics

Securing grants can be a game-changer for your nonprofit's financial health, providing critical funding that can propel your mission forward. However, successfully obtaining grants requires careful planning, persistence, and relationship-building. The process begins with thorough research into available grant opportunities. Online databases such as Foundation Directory Online and Grants.gov serve as invaluable tools in identifying potential funders whose priorities align with your organization's mission, geographic focus, and program areas.

Beyond research, establishing relationships with funders is a vital step that many organizations overlook. Funders are more likely to support nonprofits that take the time to understand their priorities and engage in meaningful conversations. Reach out to foundation representatives with thoughtful questions and attend networking events, grant workshops, and webinars to gain insights into their expectations. Personal connections can make a difference in the highly competitive grant landscape.

Once you have identified promising opportunities and built rapport with funders, the next step is crafting a compelling grant proposal. A well-structured proposal begins with an executive summary—a concise, one-page overview that highlights your organization's mission, the specific problem you aim to address, and how grant funding will drive measurable impact.

Following the summary, develop a strong need statement that clearly outlines the community challenge your project seeks to solve. Use data, real-life examples, and testimonials to illustrate the urgency of the issue. Next, articulate your goals and objectives with clarity, specifying measurable outcomes that will demonstrate success. A detailed program description should provide a roadmap of activities, timelines, and key stakeholders involved.

A grant proposal is incomplete without a well-defined budget. Funders want to see exactly how their contributions will be allocated, so be transparent about costs, breaking down expenses in a clear, organized format. Additionally, a sustainability plan is essential—it reassures funders that your program will continue to thrive beyond the grant period. Outline strategies for future funding, partnerships, or earned income that will support long-term viability.

Evaluation is another critical component of the proposal. Funders want assurance that their investment will yield tangible results. Detail your methods for tracking progress, measuring impact, and reporting outcomes. Establish key performance indicators (KPIs) that will help assess the program's effectiveness and adapt as needed.

When it comes time to submit your grant, precision is key. Carefully follow all funder guidelines regarding formatting, attachments, and submission deadlines. Avoid last-minute technical issues by submitting well in advance.

After submission, proactive follow-up can further demonstrate your commitment. If awarded, honor the trust funders place in you by adhering to reporting requirements and keeping them informed of your program's progress. If your proposal is declined, don't be discouraged—request feedback to strengthen future applications. Each grant cycle offers valuable learning experiences that refine your approach and enhance your organization's chances of securing funding in the future.

Donor Relationships and Stewardship

Building lasting donor relationships is not just about securing financial support; it is about fostering a deep sense of belonging and shared purpose. Effective stewardship means not only thanking donors but also making them feel like integral members of your mission-driven community. The first step in this process is prompt acknowledgment. Sending thank-you emails or handwritten letters within 24-48 hours of receiving a donation demonstrates appreciation and attentiveness. A generic thank-you note is not enough—personalize your message by referencing the specific impact their gift will have on your programs or beneficiaries. A heartfelt expression of gratitude can leave a lasting impression and strengthen the emotional connection between donors and your organization.

Beyond the initial thank-you, meaningful engagement must be ongoing. Regular communication through newsletters, social media updates, and personalized outreach helps donors see the tangible results of their contributions. Share compelling stories that highlight the real-life impact of their generosity. Featuring testimonials from beneficiaries, behind-the-scenes glimpses of your work, and updates on key initiatives can help donors feel invested in the progress of your mission. To deepen their involvement, consider offering exclusive experiences such as behind-the-scenes tours, invitation-only events, or access to special reports and donor-exclusive webinars. When donors feel connected to your cause beyond their financial contributions, they are more likely to remain committed supporters.

Stewardship is also a data-driven endeavor. Understanding donor preferences, interests, and giving history allows you to tailor your outreach and create a more meaningful connection. Utilize a donor management system to track interactions and segment your donor list so that communications feel personalized rather than one-size-fits-all. A well-organized stewardship calendar can help ensure consistency, mapping out key engagement touchpoints such as personalized birthday greetings, holiday messages, and check-in calls from staff or board members.

Measuring donor retention and loyalty is essential to refining your engagement strategies. Track key performance indicators such as donor retention rate and donor lifetime value (DLV) to gauge the effectiveness of your efforts. Analyzing trends in giving behavior can help you identify donors who may be at risk of disengaging, allowing you to intervene with thoughtful re-engagement strategies before they lapse. Building trust through transparency, ongoing gratitude, and genuine connection ensures that donors see themselves not just as contributors, but as valued partners in your nonprofit's long-term success. By cultivating these relationships with care and intention, you create a loyal donor base that will sustain and champion your mission for years to come.me.

Staffing and Volunteer Management

When (and How) to Hire Staff: Deciding When to Bring on Employees vs. Contractors

Deciding when to hire staff is one of the most pivotal moments in the life of a nonprofit. It's not just about filling a position—it's about strategically expanding your organization's reach, strengthening its capacity, and ensuring that every new addition aligns with your mission. Bringing someone new into your organization isn't just about meeting an immediate need; it's about building for the future, fostering a sustainable work environment, and ensuring that every hire is contributing to the greater vision of your nonprofit.

Imagine this: Your nonprofit has been making steady progress, and your mission is gaining traction. The demand for your services is growing, but so is the workload. Your current team is stretched thin, working long hours to keep up. You're caught between maintaining momentum and avoiding burnout. This is the moment every nonprofit leader faces—the critical decision of whether to hire full-time staff or seek external support through contractors. The weight of this choice is immense because it doesn't just affect the financial bottom line; it directly impacts your organization's ability to sustain its mission, maintain efficiency, and cultivate a strong internal culture.

On one hand, hiring a full-time employee brings stability, continuity, and a long-term commitment to your mission. Employees become deeply embedded in the culture and operations of the organization, contributing not just their skills but their passion and dedication. On the other hand, contractors offer flexibility, specialized expertise, and a cost-effective solution for short-term projects or fluctuating workloads. But how do you decide? Understanding the nuances of each option is essential to making the right choice, and a well-informed decision will set your nonprofit up for success in the long run.

Knowing When It's Time to Hire

Before expanding your team, take a moment to step back and assess the bigger picture. Imagine standing at a crossroads—one path leads to pushing through with your current capacity, while the other opens doors to new possibilities through strategic growth. Is your team constantly playing catch-up? Are critical deadlines slipping through the cracks? Are there specialized skills you desperately need but lack internally? These are the signs that it may be time to bring in additional support.

Hiring employees is not just a transaction—it's a long-term commitment to the stability and growth of your organization. Employees become the backbone of your nonprofit, embedded in its mission, culture, and daily operations. They bring continuity, build relationships, and ensure that institutional knowledge remains within the organization. However, hiring full-time staff also means taking on the financial responsibility of salaries, benefits, and employment taxes.

On the other hand, contractors provide a different kind of solution. They bring in specialized skills and offer flexibility that a permanent hire may not. If you need expertise in a particular area—like grant writing, graphic design, or event planning—but don't require that role on a daily basis, a contractor can fill that gap without the long-term financial commitment. Think of contractors as skilled specialists who come in to solve specific challenges before moving on to the next opportunity. Knowing when to hire an employee versus a contractor is crucial in maintaining both financial health and operational efficiency.

How to Decide: Employee vs. Contractor

An employee is more than just a worker; they are a long-term investment in your nonprofit's mission and culture. They become woven into the fabric of your organization, bringing consistency, dedication, and institutional knowledge. Employees are on your payroll, receive benefits, and operate under employment laws, making them ideal for roles that require ongoing, stable support.

Contractors, on the other hand, function as external specialists brought in for specific tasks or projects. They are independent professionals responsible for their own taxes and benefits, and they operate with a greater degree of autonomy. Unlike employees, contractors work within the scope of defined projects, meeting deadlines and delivering results without becoming embedded in the daily operations of your nonprofit.

If your organization is growing and requires ongoing support in essential areas such as fundraising, operations, or program management, hiring an employee ensures continuity and integration into your long-term vision. Employees are particularly valuable in roles that demand deep understanding, relationship-building, and sustained effort.

However, if your nonprofit is undergoing a temporary transition—like launching a rebranding campaign, organizing an annual gala, or developing a strategic plan— a contractor's specialized skills and flexibility make them an excellent choice. Contractors allow you to access high-level expertise without the financial and operational commitments that come with permanent staff, ensuring that your organization can adapt quickly to changing needs while keeping costs in check.

Steps to Hire Successfully

Once you've made the pivotal decision to hire, the real work begins—planning meticulously to ensure success. Hiring isn't just about filling a role; it's about crafting a thoughtful and strategic approach that aligns with your nonprofit's goals. The first step is writing a compelling and detailed job description, one that not only outlines responsibilities, required skills, and expectations but also reflects the mission and culture of your organization. A well-crafted job description is your first opportunity to attract the right candidates who will be a great fit for both the role and your team.

For contractors, this process takes a different form. Instead of a traditional job description, you'll need a thorough and precise contract that outlines project scope, deliverables, deadlines, and payment terms. Transparency in agreements ensures that both parties have clear expectations, reducing misunderstandings down the road.

Equally important is ensuring compliance with legal and financial regulations. Misclassifying employees as contractors—or vice versa—can lead to costly penalties and unnecessary complications. Taking the time to review IRS guidelines and state labor laws will save you from potential headaches and reinforce your organization's credibility. With proper planning and foresight, your hiring process will not only bring in the right talent but also strengthen your nonprofit's foundation for long-term success.

Onboarding and Retention: Practical Onboarding Steps

Hiring the right person is only the beginning of the journey. The true test of success lies in how well they integrate into the organization, how supported they feel, and how quickly they can contribute to your nonprofit's mission. The moment a new hire steps through the door, they bring with them a mix of excitement, anticipation, and perhaps even nervous energy. This is your opportunity to harness that enthusiasm and transform it into deep engagement and commitment.

A well-crafted onboarding experience isn't merely a procedural step—it's an immersive introduction to the heart and soul of your nonprofit. It's about ensuring that every new team member feels a sense of belonging from the very first day, that they understand their role in the larger mission, and that they are equipped with the tools and knowledge necessary to succeed. More than policies and procedures, onboarding should be a warm welcome, an invitation into a community, and a structured path toward making an impact. Organizations that invest in thoughtful onboarding don't just improve retention—they create a culture of loyalty, enthusiasm, and passion, fostering employees who are not just workers but true advocates for the cause.

Before They Walk in the Door

The onboarding process begins well before the employee's first day—it's about more than just paperwork and logistics. It's the first step in shaping their experience, setting the tone for their journey with your organization, and making them feel truly welcomed. A well-prepared onboarding plan signals to new hires that they are valued, that their contributions matter, and that their success is important to the nonprofit's mission.

Imagine walking into a new job and being greeted with an organized plan, a clear understanding of your role, and the tools you need to hit the ground running. That's the experience you want to create for your new team member. Before their first day, ensure they receive a thoughtful welcome email outlining what to expect in their first week. Provide them with access to key policy documents, technology systems, and an introduction to team communication channels. Make sure their email, software accounts, and workspace are not just ready but personalized to reflect their role and how they will contribute to the team.

These small yet meaningful steps show that you're not just bringing them on board to fill a role but inviting them into a mission-driven community where they can thrive. A well-prepared onboarding experience instills confidence, fosters connection, and ultimately lays the groundwork for long-term engagement and success.

Day One and First Impressions

First impressions are powerful—they shape a new hire's sense of belonging and enthusiasm from the very start. From the moment they step into your nonprofit—whether physically walking through the doors or logging into their first virtual meeting—they should feel an immediate sense of welcome and purpose. It's about making them feel like they're stepping into a community, not just an organization.

Consider beginning their first day with an intentional, warm introduction to the team. Whether it's a casual meet-and-greet over coffee, a personal welcome message from leadership, or a thoughtfully planned welcome package, these small gestures make a big impact. Share the story behind your nonprofit's mission, not just as a presentation but as an engaging conversation. Help them see that they are stepping into something larger than themselves, that their role has real meaning, and that their contributions will shape the future of the cause they are joining.

Avoid overwhelming them with an immediate avalanche of policies and procedures. Instead, create a comfortable atmosphere where they can ease into their new role. Give them space to absorb information, encourage them to ask questions, and set up structured opportunities for them to connect with their new colleagues. The goal is to replace any first-day anxiety with excitement, curiosity, and a sense of connection. A well-thought-out first day isn't just about checking boxes; it's about sparking inspiration and making new hires feel they are exactly where they're meant to be.

The First 30 Days

The first month is a critical period of transition, where excitement and nerves intertwine as a new hire finds their place within the organization. Think of it as laying the foundation for long-term success—what happens in these first few weeks can shape an employee's engagement, confidence, and productivity for months to come.

Start by scheduling regular one-on-one check-ins with supervisors and colleagues. These meetings should be more than just routine status updates; they should serve as opportunities for meaningful conversations, where new hires feel safe to share their thoughts, voice concerns, and ask questions. These interactions are pivotal in fostering a sense of belonging. It's in these moments—whether over a coffee chat, a virtual call, or a quick team huddle—that a new hire starts to feel like an integral part of the organization, rather than just another employee.

To keep them engaged and motivated, introduce short-term learning goals that allow them to see immediate progress and celebrate small wins. Think of these as stepping stones that guide them through their first few weeks, building confidence along the way. Whether it's mastering a new software tool, leading a small project, or successfully navigating their first team meeting, these achievements reinforce a sense of accomplishment. A new hire who experiences growth early on will feel more invested in their role and more inspired to stay committed to the journey ahead. By giving them a roadmap with clear, attainable goals, you not only set them up for success but also cultivate a sense of purpose and excitement about their future within the organization.

Retention Starts on Day One

People stay where they feel seen, heard, and appreciated. Beyond the initial onboarding process, the key to retaining passionate and committed employees is to cultivate a workplace culture that fosters growth, acknowledges contributions, and provides meaningful opportunities for development. Employees who feel valued are not just more likely to stay—they are also more engaged, motivated, and invested in the mission of your nonprofit.

One of the simplest yet most effective ways to keep employees engaged is through recognition. Taking the time to celebrate individual and team accomplishments— whether through a formal recognition program like "Employee of the Month" or small but meaningful gestures like personalized thank-you notes or verbal acknowledgments in team meetings—can significantly boost morale. These moments of appreciation reinforce that each team member's work has an impact and is genuinely valued.

But appreciation alone is not enough; employees also need opportunities for professional growth. Providing access to mentorship, training programs, and career advancement paths helps them see a future within the organization. Encouraging employees to take on new challenges, lead projects, or develop new skills not only benefits them but also strengthens the nonprofit as a whole.

Another vital piece of long-term engagement is ensuring employees feel truly heard and valued. A workplace where people feel their voices matter is one where they invest their passion, creativity, and energy. To foster this, leaders must go beyond just collecting feedback—they must actively listen, respond thoughtfully, and take meaningful action based on what they hear. Whether through anonymous surveys, one-on-one check-ins, or open forums, providing multiple avenues for employees to share their experiences creates a culture of trust and transparency.

When employees witness real changes stemming from their input—whether it's improved workflow processes, enhanced benefits, or a shift in communication strategies—they don't just feel heard; they feel like integral architects of the organization's growth. This sense of ownership deepens their connection to the mission and strengthens their commitment to its success. Retention isn't just about competitive salaries or perks; it's about respect, recognition, and fostering an environment where every employee knows they matter and their contributions help shape the future of the organization.

How to Build a Volunteer Program: Managing and Retaining Volunteers Effectively

Volunteers are the heartbeat of many nonprofits, infusing organizations with fresh energy, diverse skills, and an unshakable passion for the mission. They arrive with enthusiasm, eager to make a difference, whether by offering their time, talents, or unique perspectives. However, recruiting volunteers is just the beginning of the journey. The real challenge—and the true measure of a successful volunteer program—is keeping them engaged, inspired, and committed for the long haul. Volunteers who feel valued, connected, and appreciated don't just contribute; they become ambassadors for your cause, bringing others along with them and deepening the impact of your organization.

Designing a Volunteer Program That Works

Before you begin recruiting volunteers, take a step back and assess where their support is most needed. Are they best suited to help with daily operations, assist with major fundraising events, or lend their expertise to special projects? Each volunteer role should have a clear and compelling description that not only outlines the time commitment and responsibilities but also highlights the meaningful impact they will have on your organization's mission. Volunteers should be able to see themselves as an integral part of your team, rather than just extra hands to help when needed.

Additionally, it's important to have a system in place to track volunteer hours and activities. Not only does this allow you to acknowledge and appreciate their contributions, but it also provides tangible data that can be used for reporting to funders, measuring the effectiveness of your volunteer program, and strengthening grant applications. Showing volunteers that their time and dedication are making a real impact helps build long-term commitment and keeps them engaged in your mission.

Recruiting Volunteers

Recruitment is about more than just finding people—it's about reaching them where they already are and showing them why your cause matters. Volunteers come from all walks of life, each with their own reasons for wanting to give back, so your outreach efforts should be as diverse and engaging as the people you hope to attract. Utilize social media to share compelling stories and showcase the impact volunteers can have. Tap into local community boards and partner with organizations that align with your mission to broaden your reach. Host virtual and in-person information sessions where potential volunteers can ask questions and see firsthand how they can contribute.

To make getting involved as seamless and inviting as possible, create a dedicated volunteer portal on your website—one that doesn't just function as a sign-up form but serves as a warm and engaging entryway into your organization's community. Think of it as a digital welcome center, offering potential volunteers a sense of what it truly means to be part of your mission.

Instead of merely listing available opportunities, bring them to life. Share compelling stories of current volunteers and the real-world impact they've made. Provide clear, detailed descriptions of different roles so people can see exactly where their skills and passions might fit. Include a FAQ section to address common concerns and help ease any hesitation someone may have before signing up. The more transparent and accessible you make the process, the more comfortable and motivated people will feel about taking that first step.

A well-designed volunteer portal should be a place where people don't just sign up, but where they feel inspired, informed, and excited to get involved. By creating a space that feels welcoming, inclusive, and informative, you're not just recruiting volunteers—you're building a community of passionate changemakers who feel connected to your cause from the very beginning.

Onboarding Volunteers

Volunteers are not just extra hands; they are an essential part of your mission. Treat them with the same care and intentionality as you would employees. Start with a comprehensive orientation that not only walks them through the logistics of their role but immerses them in the heart of your organization. Share the story of your nonprofit, introduce them to key team members, and highlight the real impact their work will have on the community. This helps them feel connected and motivated from day one.

Training is not just about instruction—it's about empowerment, confidence, and ensuring that volunteers feel prepared and supported in their roles. Imagine stepping into a new environment, eager to contribute but unsure of what's expected or how to navigate your responsibilities. That uncertainty can be daunting, which is why a strong training program is essential for creating a sense of ease and belonging.

Volunteers should feel equipped not only with the knowledge they need to perform their tasks but also with a deeper understanding of how their efforts contribute to the larger mission. Whether they are assisting at an event, working behind the scenes, or providing direct services, each volunteer should know that their work is valuable and impactful.

Creating an engaging and hands-on training experience helps build confidence from the start. Instead of just handing out a manual, incorporate interactive sessions, shadowing opportunities, and real-time feedback. Encourage questions, foster collaboration, and reassure volunteers that they have access to ongoing support whenever they need it. When volunteers feel prepared and valued, they become more than just helpers—they become invested advocates for your cause.

Ensuring the safety and clarity of your volunteer program starts with gathering the right information. By having volunteers complete applications and liability waivers, you not only create an organized system but also lay the foundation for trust and accountability. Collecting emergency contacts, setting clear expectations, and addressing legal considerations are crucial steps in safeguarding both your volunteers and your organization.

These steps go beyond mere formalities—they signal to volunteers that their well-being is a priority. When people feel that their time and contributions are valued, they are more likely to engage deeply with your mission. Taking the time to make the process transparent and thoughtful shows that your nonprofit isn't just looking for extra hands;

you are inviting dedicated individuals into a structured, supportive, and rewarding experience. A well-organized volunteer program fosters confidence, ensuring that those who step forward to serve do so with enthusiasm, security, and a strong sense of belonging.

Keeping Volunteers Engaged

The best volunteers are those who return, time and time again, driven by a sense of purpose and belonging. To cultivate that level of engagement, it's crucial to offer roles that fit into their lives. Some volunteers may only have time for short-term projects, while others may be looking for ongoing commitments where they can build deeper connections and take on greater responsibility. Meeting volunteers where they are ensures they stay motivated and continue to contribute in ways that feel fulfilling to them.

Keeping volunteers engaged doesn't end after their initial training—it requires ongoing communication and support. Regular check-ins, whether informal chats or structured meetings, provide a valuable opportunity to hear their thoughts and experiences firsthand. Ask them what aspects of their work they enjoy most, where they see room for improvement, and what challenges they may be facing. Volunteers who feel heard and supported are far more likely to remain committed. Taking their feedback seriously and implementing meaningful changes not only strengthens your volunteer program but also fosters a culture of collaboration and appreciation. When volunteers see that their voices matter, they develop a stronger emotional investment in your mission, making them more likely to stay for the long haul.

Recognizing and Retaining Volunteers

Recognition is the glue that binds volunteers to your mission, reinforcing their sense of belonging and purpose. A heartfelt thank-you goes a long way, but true appreciation extends beyond words—it's about making volunteers feel seen, valued, and integral to your nonprofit's success. Hosting a volunteer appreciation event is a wonderful way to celebrate their contributions, whether it's a casual gathering, a heartfelt awards ceremony, or a handwritten note expressing gratitude for their time and dedication. Publicly acknowledging their impact—whether through social media shoutouts, newsletters, or a feature during National Volunteer Week—helps them see the difference they are making.

However, recognition isn't just about celebrating the present; it's about fostering future growth. Volunteers want to feel like their work is meaningful, and one of the best ways to keep them engaged is by providing opportunities for development. Encourage them to take on leadership roles, mentor new volunteers, or spearhead special projects. When volunteers see a clear path to grow within your organization, they become more invested, deepening their commitment and connection. A thriving volunteer program is built on both gratitude and growth—when volunteers feel valued and empowered, they won't just stay; they'll inspire others to join as well.

Measuring Volunteer Impact

Tracking volunteer hours and impact is more than just a logistical necessity—it's a way to highlight the real, tangible difference volunteers make in advancing your mission. Every hour contributed, every task completed, and every milestone achieved builds a compelling narrative that resonates with donors, funders, and the volunteers themselves.

When volunteers see their efforts making a measurable impact, their sense of purpose deepens. By sharing these stories—whether in newsletters, social media posts, or donor reports—you help paint a vivid picture of how volunteers bring your mission to life. A testimonial from a volunteer who witnessed firsthand the change they helped create, a photo of a community event powered by their dedication, or a heartfelt thank-you message from a beneficiary all serve as powerful reminders that their time and effort truly matter.

People are drawn to stories that showcase real transformation. By capturing and sharing these moments, you not only inspire continued volunteer engagement but also strengthen the support of funders who want to invest in meaningful change. Volunteers don't just want to help; they want to see the ripple effect of their work—and it's your role to make sure they do.

By understanding the right time to bring in employees or contractors, crafting a welcoming and supportive onboarding experience, and fostering a thriving volunteer program, you set the stage for your nonprofit's success. At the core of your organization are the people who give their time, talent, and dedication—employees, contractors, and volunteers alike. They are not just the workforce behind your mission; they are its heartbeat, its advocates, and its most passionate supporters. When you invest in them—by listening, recognizing their efforts, and providing opportunities for growth—you create a ripple effect that strengthens your entire organization. Take care of your people, and in return, they will champion your cause, ensuring that your mission continues to grow and make a lasting impact in the communities you serve.

Marketing and Communications for Nonprofits

Building Your Brand and Voice

Every nonprofit has a story to tell, and your brand is the way people experience and remember that story. Think of it as the emotional and visual fingerprint of your organization— a combination of the values you hold, the message you communicate, and the way you show up in the world. Every interaction with your audience, whether through a social media post, a donor email, or an in-person event, contributes to their perception of your mission and the trust they place in you.

Building a brand is not just about aesthetics—it's about creating a lasting impression that resonates with supporters and stakeholders. A strong brand is clear, cohesive, and rooted in authenticity. It should evoke emotion, inspire action, and establish credibility. Whether through the careful selection of colors that convey your mission's essence, the words you choose to communicate impact, or the tone of your messaging, each element plays a crucial role in shaping how people connect with and support your cause. Your brand is more than just a logo—it is the soul of your nonprofit, expressed in every touchpoint.

Your logo is one of the most powerful visual representations of your nonprofit's identity. Think of it as your organization's signature, the emblem that people will come to recognize and associate with your mission. It should be a reflection of your nonprofit's essence, a symbol that tells a story at just

137

a glance. A well-designed logo is both memorable and versatile—simple enough to look sharp on everything from a billboard to a business card, yet distinctive enough to make an impression in a crowded digital landscape.

Beyond just design, color choices carry deep psychological weight. Green, for example, often conveys themes of growth, renewal, and sustainability, while blue exudes trust, stability, and professionalism. The typography you select further strengthens your brand identity—whether your organization wants to appear authoritative and formal or inviting and warm, your fonts should align with that vision.

Crafting a strong logo and visual identity doesn't have to be overwhelming. Online tools like Canva and Adobe Illustrator offer user-friendly design options, but when possible, investing in a professional designer can elevate your branding and ensure your visual identity remains polished, timeless, and reflective of your nonprofit's values.

But branding goes beyond the visual. It extends into the words you choose, the tone you set, and the personality you convey every time you communicate with the world. Your organization's voice is how you connect with your audience—will you be warm and compassionate, fostering a sense of community, or will you be bold and authoritative, positioning yourself as a leader in your field? The right tone depends on your mission, your audience, and the values you uphold.

Consistency is key to building trust and recognition. When someone reads a post on your website, sees a tweet, or opens one of your emails, they should immediately recognize the voice as distinctly yours. This familiarity fosters connection and credibility, making it easier for your supporters to engage with your work and advocate on your behalf.

To maintain this clarity and cohesion, developing a messaging guide is invaluable. This guide serves as a roadmap for staff and volunteers, ensuring that every piece of communication—whether an official statement, a donor appeal, or a simple social media caption—aligns with your nonprofit's core identity. When everyone within the organization speaks in unison, the message becomes stronger, more impactful, and ultimately more effective in advancing your mission.

Storytelling for Social Impact

People are moved to action by stories, not statistics. Numbers may illustrate a need, but it is the lived experiences of individuals that stir emotions, inspire generosity, and create lasting engagement. Nonprofits understand this power well, which is why storytelling should be at the heart of every communication effort. Instead of leading with data points or program descriptions, focus on the human lives that have been transformed by your work. A volunteer whose perspective has been reshaped, a donor who found deeper purpose through giving, or a beneficiary whose life took a turn for the better—these are the stories that resonate.

Every compelling story follows a journey. Introduce your hero, someone who faced a challenge or hardship before crossing paths with your nonprofit. Illustrate their struggle vividly, allowing your audience to feel their frustration, pain, or uncertainty. Then, introduce the turning point—the moment when your nonprofit's support changed their trajectory. Show, in real and tangible ways, how their life began to transform. Was it a scholarship that allowed them to finish their education? A mentor who gave them hope? A shelter that provided safety? Finally, bring the story full circle. Paint a picture of their "happily ever after"—the lasting impact of your organization's work. Have they regained stability? Found a renewed sense of purpose? Become an advocate for others in similar situations? The resolution should leave your audience inspired and motivated to take action.

Visual elements breathe life into storytelling, transforming abstract concepts into vivid, emotional experiences. A single photograph can freeze a moment in time, capturing raw emotions that words alone might struggle to convey. A well-produced video can immerse viewers in a person's journey, allowing them to hear their voice, witness their struggles, and celebrate their triumphs. These visuals create an immediate and lasting impact, strengthening the connection between your audience and your mission.

But powerful visuals don't stand alone—they must be paired with compelling narratives. A poignant image of a child receiving their first book means more when the audience understands the obstacles they overcame to reach that moment. A short video showcasing volunteers in action is more moving when their motivations and the significance of their work are explained. When woven together, these elements become undeniable calls to action, compelling people to support, advocate, and engage.

To maximize the impact of your visuals, strategically feature them across multiple platforms. Showcase compelling images and videos prominently on your website to immediately draw visitors into your cause. Use them in social media campaigns to increase engagement and shareability, bringing more eyes to your work. Incorporate them into email campaigns to create deeper connections with your supporters. And above all, always provide a clear path for action—whether it's donating, volunteering, amplifying your message, or becoming an ambassador for your mission. The more your audience feels immersed in your story, the more inspired they will be to stand with you and help create change.

Social Media and Digital Outreach

Social media has evolved into one of the most powerful storytelling and engagement tools available to nonprofits. It is a dynamic space where you can bring your mission to life, illustrate your impact, and cultivate a vibrant community of supporters in real time. Unlike traditional outreach methods, social media allows for immediate interaction, giving nonprofits the opportunity to not just broadcast their work but to have meaningful conversations with those who care about their cause.

However, not all social media platforms serve the same purpose, and choosing the right ones for your organization is key. If your goal is professional networking and thought leadership, LinkedIn is an ideal space to share insights, success stories, and industry expertise. Instagram, with its visual-driven format, provides a powerful canvas for storytelling through compelling imagery and videos. Meanwhile, TikTok's short-form, highly creative content allows nonprofits to connect with younger audiences in engaging and innovative ways. The key to success is not just being present on these platforms but using them strategically to foster connection, amplify your message, and inspire action.

Effective content planning is the backbone of a successful digital strategy for nonprofits. Without a clear plan, social media efforts can feel scattered and reactive rather than strategic and impactful. By creating a content calendar, your team can ensure that posts are scheduled in advance, thoughtfully curated, and aligned with your mission. This proactive approach saves time, reduces last-minute scrambling, and ensures consistency in messaging.

A well-balanced content strategy should include a variety of engaging posts that showcase different facets of your organization. Share inspiring stories that highlight the impact of your work, offering a human-centered perspective that resonates emotionally with your audience. Give a behind-the-scenes look at the daily efforts of your staff and volunteers, offering transparency and authenticity. Celebrate your supporters by showcasing volunteer highlights and donor appreciation posts. And don't shy away from direct calls to action—whether it's an urgent fundraising appeal, an event invitation, or a request for volunteers, clear CTAs drive engagement and deepen audience investment.

However, social media isn't just about broadcasting your message—it's about fostering connections. Engagement is key. Go beyond simply posting by actively interacting with your audience. Reply to comments and messages, answer questions thoughtfully, and engage in conversations that align with your mission. Hosting live events, Q&A sessions, or interactive polls can strengthen community involvement and make your supporters feel like active participants in your cause.

Tracking performance is equally important. Social media analytics provide valuable insights into what's working and what needs adjustment. By monitoring key metrics such as reach, engagement rates, click-throughs, and shares, your nonprofit can refine its strategy and ensure that your digital presence remains compelling and effective.

Email marketing is a cornerstone of digital outreach, providing a direct and personal way to connect with supporters. Your email list isn't just a collection of contacts—it represents individuals who believe in your mission and want to stay informed and engaged. Every email you send is an opportunity to strengthen relationships, deepen commitment, and inspire action.

More than just a newsletter, email campaigns allow you to share impactful stories, celebrate successes, and provide meaningful updates on your work. A compelling email should feel like a conversation, drawing readers in with relatable narratives and a clear call to action. Whether it's an invitation to an upcoming event, a heartfelt thank-you to donors, or a spotlight on a beneficiary whose life has changed, each email should serve a purpose and reinforce your mission.

Using tools like Mailchimp and Constant Contact, nonprofits can easily craft visually appealing and mobile-friendly emails that captivate readers. A well-segmented email list ensures that the right messages reach the right audiences—whether it's major donors, volunteers, or general supporters. By maintaining a consistent and engaging email presence, your nonprofit can cultivate lasting connections and drive meaningful engagement.

Media Relations and PR

The media can be a powerful amplifier for your nonprofit's mission, bringing your cause to a wider audience and helping to build credibility. But earning media coverage isn't just about having a great story—it's about understanding how to strategically position that story so that it resonates with journalists and their audiences. Relationships are at the heart of successful media outreach. Start by identifying reporters and bloggers who regularly cover nonprofit issues, community affairs, or the specific cause your organization addresses. Take the time to engage with their work—read their articles, comment on their social media posts, and build a rapport before you ever send them a pitch. A well-maintained media list—a living document of reporters' names, email addresses, publication focuses, and past interactions—will help you stay organized and ready when an opportunity arises.

When you have news to share, such as a grant award, an upcoming event, or a milestone in your organization's journey, a press release is a structured way to get the word out. A strong press release follows a clear format: a compelling headline, a lead paragraph answering the essential questions (who, what, when, where, and why), followed by supporting details, quotes from key stakeholders, and a brief boilerplate about your nonprofit. Enhancing your release with high-resolution images, relevant statistics, and clear contact information increases the likelihood of coverage, making it easier for journalists to craft a story around your announcement.

For feature stories or more in-depth coverage, a well-crafted pitch is key. Instead of sending a generic email blast, tailor your pitch to each journalist's beat and interests. Research what they've written about recently and find a way to connect your story to larger trends or current events. The more relevant and timely your pitch, the more likely it is to grab their attention. If a journalist expresses interest, be prepared. Have an articulate spokesperson—whether it's your executive director, a program leader, or a beneficiary of your services—who can confidently convey your message. Investing in media training for key figures within your organization ensures they can handle interviews effectively, avoid common pitfalls, and present your nonprofit's story in the most compelling and impactful way possible.

Dashboards: Communicating Data to Boards, Stakeholders, and Funders

Numbers tell a story, but without the right tools, they can become overwhelming, buried in spreadsheets and dense reports. That's where dashboards become invaluable. A well-designed dashboard serves as a bridge between raw data and meaningful insight, transforming complex information into an engaging, visual representation of progress. For board members, stakeholders, and funders, a dashboard provides a clear and immediate snapshot of impact, helping them understand how resources are being utilized and what progress is being made toward organizational goals.

Before you embark on creating a dashboard, take the time to determine which metrics truly matter. What story do you want to tell? For funders, financial sustainability and measurable program impact are often at the forefront. For staff and leadership, operational efficiency, donor engagement, and community reach may be top priorities. By identifying these key data points, you ensure that your dashboard remains focused and meaningful rather than overwhelming with unnecessary information.

Once the right metrics are established, selecting the appropriate tool becomes the next step. Advanced platforms like Power BI, Tableau, and Google Data Studio offer robust analytics and visualization capabilities, allowing nonprofits to create interactive dashboards with real-time updates. However, for organizations with simpler needs, even a well-structured Excel sheet with charts and graphs can be an effective means of presenting data. The goal is not just to collect numbers but to make them accessible, actionable, and impactful.

Design plays a crucial role in making data both understandable and engaging. A well-structured dashboard should be visually intuitive, allowing users to grasp key insights at a glance. Simple yet effective visuals such as bar charts, line graphs, and pie charts can transform complex numbers into a compelling narrative. Each chart or graph should serve a purpose, making trends and patterns instantly recognizable rather than overwhelming the viewer with excessive data points.

Color-coding is another powerful tool that enhances clarity and quick comprehension. By using universally understood indicators—such as green for progress, yellow for caution, and red for areas needing improvement—you can create an immediate visual cue that highlights performance against set goals. This method allows stakeholders to quickly assess where efforts are succeeding and where adjustments may be necessary.

Equally important is ensuring accessibility and usability. A dashboard should not be cluttered or difficult to navigate; it should be structured in a way that guides the user seamlessly from one insight to the next. Whether shared as a downloadable PDF or an interactive online tool, it should be easy to interpret, regardless of technical expertise.

Thoughtfully designed dashboards empower leadership, staff, and funders to make informed decisions based on clear, visualized data that tells a meaningful story.

Don't just send dashboards—bring them to life with context and storytelling. When presenting data to your board, go beyond the numbers and illuminate the narrative behind them. Data alone can seem dry or overwhelming, but when paired with thoughtful analysis, it becomes a compelling testament to your nonprofit's progress. If a dashboard reflects an uptick in donations following a specific event, don't just highlight the increase—dive into what made that event so effective. Was it a heartfelt keynote speech that resonated with attendees? A strategic social media campaign that broadened your reach? Or perhaps a new donor engagement approach that strengthened relationships? By connecting the numbers to real-world actions and outcomes, you help stakeholders see the bigger picture, reinforcing the impact of their support and guiding future decision-making with clarity and purpose.

Conclusion

Marketing and communications are the heartbeat of nonprofit growth, pulsing through every interaction, campaign, and outreach effort. Your brand is the foundation of how the world perceives you—more than just a logo or tagline, it's the story you tell, the trust you build, and the emotions you evoke. Compelling storytelling breathes life into your mission, transforming abstract ideas into powerful narratives that inspire action. Through social media, you create a two-way street of engagement, not just broadcasting updates but cultivating conversations, relationships, and community. Media coverage elevates your credibility, extending your reach and reinforcing the importance of your work. And dashboards, often overlooked in their significance, provide the clarity and transparency that donors, stakeholders, and board members need to see the tangible impact of their support. When woven together, these elements create a powerful ecosystem of communication that strengthens your nonprofit's ability to make a lasting difference, build meaningful connections, and drive sustainable growth.

Launching Your First Programs and Events

Every nonprofit founder dreams of the day their mission transforms from an idea into tangible action. It's a moment of profound realization—when the hard work, passion, and vision coalesce into something real, something that touches lives and begins to effect change. You may have spent months, maybe even years, conceptualizing your mission, refining your goals, and rallying support. And now, you stand at the precipice of actually bringing your work to the people who need it most.

But turning that dream into action can feel overwhelming. The excitement is often paired with an onslaught of questions. Where do you even begin? How do you create something sustainable and impactful? What if it doesn't work? These concerns are valid, and every nonprofit leader has faced them at some point. The key is to approach the journey with both strategy and adaptability.

This chapter will walk you through the crucial steps needed to turn your mission into meaningful programs and events that truly make a difference. You'll learn how to develop initiatives that align with your goals, organize events that engage and inspire, and measure your impact to ensure that your efforts lead to lasting change. By the end, you'll not only have a clearer understanding of how to bring your vision to life, but also the confidence to take that first leap forward.

Turning Your Mission Into Action: Developing Your First Programs

Imagine standing in a community center, the hum of eager voices filling the air as young students gather, their eyes wide with curiosity and anticipation. It's the first day of your nonprofit's mentorship program, and the energy in the room is electric. The walls are adorned with bright posters displaying inspirational quotes, and the smell of fresh notebooks and sharpened pencils fills the space. Volunteers and mentors exchange warm smiles as they prepare to welcome their mentees. You take a deep breath, feeling both the weight of responsibility and the immense joy of seeing your vision come to life.

But this moment didn't happen by accident. It took months of careful planning, deep conversations with community members, and strategic partnerships to ensure that today would be a success. You spent hours refining the curriculum, training mentors, and securing a welcoming space where students could feel supported and empowered. You rallied local businesses to donate supplies and reached out to schools to identify students who would benefit most from the program.

Now, as you stand before these young minds, you realize that this is just the beginning. The true impact of your program will unfold in the weeks and months ahead as students gain confidence, develop new skills, and form meaningful relationships with their mentors. The journey to get here may have been long, but the potential for change makes every challenge worthwhile. Here's how you can embark on this journey and create a program that transforms lives.

1. Start with a Needs Assessment

Before you even think about the details of your program, take a step back and immerse yourself in the community you seek to serve. Close your eyes and picture the people whose lives you want to impact. What are their daily struggles? What keeps them up at night? What resources do they desperately need but lack access to? The answers to these questions will shape the foundation of your program.

Conducting a needs assessment is like mapping out an unfamiliar journey. Without it, you risk heading in the wrong direction, pouring valuable time and resources into solutions that may not address the actual problems. Start by engaging directly with the community—hold open forums, distribute surveys, and sit down with individuals to listen to their stories. Pay attention not just to what is being said, but also to what remains unspoken. Observe patterns, gaps, and recurring themes.

For instance, if your mission is to provide mentorship to youth, don't assume their primary struggle is academics. Dig deeper—perhaps they are facing social isolation, lack of parental support, or difficulty accessing career guidance. Understanding these nuances will enable you to design a program that meets their real needs, not just what you initially perceived as their challenges.

A well-executed needs assessment isn't just about gathering data—it's about building trust. When people see that you are truly listening, they become invested in the process, making them more likely to engage with and support your initiative. This foundational work sets the stage for programs that truly make a difference, ensuring that every step you take is guided by real insights rather than assumptions.

2. Design Your Program

Once you have a clear understanding of what's needed, you can begin crafting the framework of your program, much like an architect meticulously drafting the blueprint for a house. Without a strong plan in place, you risk constructing something unstable, something that might collapse under the weight of unforeseen challenges. The key to success lies in specificity—defining the program's purpose with absolute clarity.

Picture yourself sitting at a desk, a blank sheet of paper before you. What is the ultimate goal of your program? Is it to help children improve their literacy skills? If so, how will you measure success? Maybe it's by increasing their reading scores by 15% over six months or ensuring that every participant reads a set number of books. Having concrete, measurable objectives helps you chart a clear course forward.

Now, break the journey into smaller, manageable steps. Will you organize weekly reading sessions in local libraries, pair students with dedicated mentors, or facilitate interactive workshops to make learning more engaging? Each of these components acts as a brick in the foundation of your program. Carefully placing each piece, reinforcing it with structured timelines and necessary resources, ensures that your program isn't just a well-intended idea, but a reality capable of transforming lives.

It's also crucial to create a realistic budget, one that acts as a guiding force rather than an afterthought. Imagine pouring your heart and soul into launching a transformative program, only to find yourself short on resources halfway through. That moment of realization—when enthusiasm meets financial roadblocks—can be devastating. To prevent this, start by mapping out every financial component, from securing a suitable space that fosters engagement to ensuring that all necessary materials are available. Consider the human element as well—the dedicated volunteers, staff, and community members who will bring your vision to life. Whether it's stipends for facilitators, transportation costs, or promotional materials, each detail must be accounted for to avoid last-minute crises. A well-planned budget not only keeps your program afloat but also builds trust with funders and partners who want to see that their contributions are being used wisely.

3. Build Partnerships

If you're trying to build something meaningful all on your own, you're making the journey far more difficult than it needs to be. Partnerships are the glue that can hold your vision together and elevate it in ways you might not have imagined. Picture a local school welcoming your mentorship program with open arms, providing a safe and inspiring space for students to gather and grow. Or imagine a small, independent bookstore generously donating reading materials, easing the burden of costs while reinforcing the community's belief in your mission. These relationships aren't just transactional; they weave a network of support, trust, and shared purpose. By collaborating with others, you transform your initiative from a solitary effort into a thriving, interconnected movement that has the power to change lives on a greater scale.

4. Pilot Your Program

Before you launch on a grand scale, it's wise to start small. Think of piloting your program like a "dress rehearsal" for a play. Just as actors refine their performances, adjust their timing, and iron out any hiccups before opening night, you too have the opportunity to test your program and make necessary adjustments before committing to a full rollout.

Imagine running your mentorship program for a small group of students first. You might notice that you don't have enough volunteers to provide individualized attention, or that the learning materials aren't as engaging as you hoped. Maybe the time slot you initially chose conflicts with after-school sports, leading to lower attendance than expected. These are the types of issues that are far easier to address in a pilot phase than after you've already scaled up. By starting small, you give yourself a low-risk environment to refine your approach, gather meaningful feedback, and ensure that when you do launch at full scale, your program will be as effective and impactful as possible.

5. Launch and Monitor

Finally, the moment has arrived—it's showtime. The months of preparation, countless meetings, and dedicated planning have all led to this. But launching your program is just the beginning; the real work happens in the moments that follow. As participants engage, mentors guide, and the community responds, you must stay alert, observing the dynamics in real-time.

Imagine stepping into the room, feeling the energy and enthusiasm as the program unfolds. Students are eager, volunteers are motivated, and the structure you carefully built is now being put to the test. But not everything will go as planned, and that's okay. Adaptability is key. Keep track of attendance to measure engagement, actively seek feedback from participants and stakeholders, and document the outcomes—both the expected and the surprising ones.

If students are thriving, celebrate that success and look for ways to build on it. If challenges arise, approach them as opportunities for growth rather than setbacks. A program that evolves with the needs of its community is one that will truly make a lasting impact. Stay flexible, stay committed, and most importantly, stay connected to the people you set out to serve.

Measuring Impact: How to Show That Your Programs Are Making a Difference

Picture this: You've just wrapped up your first year of your youth mentorship program. The months of effort, the late nights refining lesson plans, the countless hours spent matching mentors with mentees—all of it has led to this moment. You're reflecting on the journey when a message pops up on your phone. It's from a parent, and their words bring a smile to your face: "My daughter's confidence has skyrocketed since joining. Thank you." In that instant, you're reminded why you embarked on this path.

It's these moments that fuel your passion, but they also serve as proof of impact—something funders and donors will want to see. While heartfelt testimonials are powerful, measurable results are what solidify your program's credibility. Tracking progress, collecting meaningful data, and sharing the outcomes of your work will not only validate your efforts but also open doors to more opportunities, funding, and support. Understanding the impact of your program allows you to refine and improve, ensuring that every child, every participant, continues to benefit in the most meaningful way possible.

1. Identify Key Metrics

Success can take many forms, and defining what it means for your program is crucial. Imagine a classroom where students who once struggled with reading now eagerly flip through books, their confidence growing with each page. Picture a community where absenteeism drops significantly because children feel engaged and supported. Envision a neighborhood where local residents actively participate in initiatives, strengthening the bonds that hold them together. These are not just abstract hopes—they are measurable outcomes that show the true impact of your efforts.

To gauge success, start by identifying specific indicators that align with your mission. Are you aiming to improve literacy rates? If so, track reading scores before and after participation. Do you want to see stronger attendance in schools? Monitor absenteeism patterns over time. Is community involvement your priority? Look at participation numbers in events and initiatives, noting any growth or patterns. By linking these metrics directly to your program's objectives, you not only create a clear framework for measurement but also ensure that your work remains aligned with the needs of those you serve.

2. Collect Data

Gathering data is an essential step in understanding the impact of your program. It can be as simple as sitting down with participants and hearing their personal stories—learning firsthand about the changes they've experienced—or as structured as running a detailed pre- and post-program survey to measure tangible improvements. Imagine a mentor in your program sharing how a once-shy student now actively participates in discussions, or a parent expressing how their child's reading skills have blossomed. These qualitative insights, combined with quantitative metrics, create a fuller picture of success.

To make data collection efficient, consider tools like Google Forms for quick and easy surveys that participants can complete on their phones or computers. For more in-depth analysis, platforms like Salesforce can help track individual progress over time, identifying patterns and areas for improvement. Regardless of the method, the key is consistency—gathering data at regular intervals ensures that you capture meaningful insights that drive growth and refinement in your program.

3. Analyze and Share Results

Analyzing data is more than just crunching numbers—it's about uncovering the story behind the statistics. Picture a student who once struggled with reading, now confidently flipping through pages with ease. That transformation is reflected in improved reading scores, and it's reinforced by the testimonials of grateful parents who have witnessed their child's growth. But numbers alone won't capture the full impact—visualizing your data through charts and graphs makes the story come alive. Funders and stakeholders don't just want to hear about change; they want to see it. Presenting your results in a compelling, digestible format allows them to connect emotionally with your mission and recognize the tangible progress your program has achieved.

4. Continuous Improvement

Your work doesn't end once the data is collected and analyzed; in many ways, it's only the beginning. Think of data as a compass, pointing you toward areas where your program can evolve and grow. If feedback reveals that students crave more one-on-one time with mentors, don't just note it—act on it. Expand mentoring sessions, tailor activities to meet individual needs, and continuously refine your approach. Successful nonprofits are those that remain flexible, listening intently to the needs of their community and making thoughtful adjustments. Improvement isn't just about fixing problems—it's about embracing a mindset of continuous learning and striving to make an even greater impact, year after year.

5. Tell Your Impact Story

Data is a powerful tool, but it is the personal stories that truly resonate. Numbers can validate your impact, but they don't stir emotions the way a firsthand account does. Imagine sharing a statistic: "80% of students improved in reading." While impressive, it lacks the personal touch that draws people in. Now picture telling the story of Jamal, a bright yet struggling fifth-grader who felt defeated every time he opened a book. Through the mentorship program, he found guidance, encouragement, and a new belief in himself. What was once frustration turned into determination, and soon, he was earning B's in reading— something he never thought possible. That transformation, that journey, is what makes people feel connected to your mission and inspired to support it. When you weave data and real-life experiences together, you create a compelling narrative that not only informs but also moves people to action.

Conclusion

Launching your first programs and events is a defining milestone in your nonprofit's journey—where your vision takes its first tangible steps into reality. It's the culmination of hard work, strategic planning, and a deep commitment to making a difference. But beyond the spreadsheets, logistics, and key performance indicators, what truly ignites change is the human connection woven through every initiative.

Imagine the moment a child gains the confidence to read aloud for the first time, the sense of empowerment in a community rallying around a shared cause, or the gratitude in the eyes of someone whose life has been touched by your efforts. These are the moments that define impact— the ones that remind us why we embarked on this journey in the first place.

With a clear plan, measurable goals, and a mindset of continuous improvement, you will transform dreams into reality. But never forget that the most compelling force behind your mission isn't just the data you collect—it's the stories you create, the lives you touch, and the change you inspire.

Compliance and Reporting

Compliance and reporting are the backbone of a well-run nonprofit, serving as the foundation of transparency, accountability, and credibility. These essential responsibilities not only keep your organization in good standing with regulatory agencies but also help build trust with donors, funders, and the communities you serve.

For many nonprofit leaders, navigating compliance requirements can feel overwhelming, especially when faced with the intricacies of IRS Form 990, donor acknowledgment obligations, and the development of an engaging annual report. However, with a structured approach and a commitment to clear and proactive communication, compliance can transform from a burdensome task into an opportunity to reinforce your organization's integrity and impact.

Think of compliance and reporting as more than just legal requirements; they are an ongoing conversation with your stakeholders. Filing accurate and timely IRS reports demonstrates fiscal responsibility, while thoughtful donor acknowledgments and comprehensive annual reports showcase your organization's achievements and the real difference your supporters help make. By embracing these key aspects of nonprofit governance, you can not only meet the necessary requirements but also use them as powerful tools to inspire confidence, attract more support, and strengthen your mission-driven work.

Filing IRS Form 990

Each year, nonprofits embark on an important responsibility: filing IRS Form 990. This document is far more than just another piece of paperwork—it serves as a public reflection of your nonprofit's transparency, governance, and financial stewardship. It provides insight into your organization's operations, ensuring that donors, grantmakers, and the IRS have a clear understanding of how funds are being managed. Filing Form 990 on time and with accuracy is not just a regulatory requirement; it is a testament to the integrity of your organization and a key tool for building public trust.

The type of Form 990 your organization must file depends on its financial standing. For smaller nonprofits with annual gross receipts of $50,000 or less, the Form 990-N, commonly referred to as the e-Postcard, is the simplest option. This brief electronic form allows small organizations to remain compliant with minimal effort. If your nonprofit falls within the range of $50,001 to $200,000 in gross receipts and holds total assets below $500,000, then Form 990-EZ is required, offering a more detailed snapshot of your organization's financial activity. Larger organizations with gross receipts exceeding $200,000 or total assets greater than $500,000 are responsible for filing the comprehensive Form 990, which requires detailed reporting on governance, compensation, fundraising efforts, and program expenditures.

Understanding which form to file and ensuring timely submission can feel like a daunting process, but it is a vital aspect of maintaining your nonprofit's good standing.

Beyond compliance, Form 990 can serve as a valuable storytelling tool, illustrating the impact your organization has made over the past year. By approaching it with diligence and strategic thinking, your nonprofit can use this required reporting to reinforce its mission and credibility in the eyes of both regulators and supporters alike.

Timing is critical when it comes to filing your Form 990. This crucial step should take place only after your annual audit has been completed, ensuring that all financial records are accurate and up to date. Once your audit confirms the integrity of your financial statements, you must submit Form 990 by the 15th day of the 5th month following the end of your fiscal year. For most organizations operating on a calendar year, this means a firm deadline of May 15. Failing to meet this deadline can result in significant penalties, with daily fines that can accumulate rapidly, especially for larger organizations. Prioritizing your audit and planning ahead for this filing will help safeguard your nonprofit's compliance and financial health.

The filing process begins with thorough preparation, ensuring that your nonprofit's financial records are organized and accurate. This requires collaborating with your finance team or accountant to review all income, expenses, and assets to confirm everything aligns with your annual audit results. Once your financials are in order, you will use IRS-approved software to complete and file Form 990, carefully reviewing every detail to avoid discrepancies or errors that could raise red flags.

While the goal is always to file on time, sometimes unexpected delays arise—whether due to a complex audit, staffing changes, or other administrative hurdles. In such cases, Form 8868 provides a crucial lifeline, granting a 6-month extension to finalize your filing and prevent costly penalties. However, this extension should be used strategically, ensuring your team remains proactive in gathering all necessary documentation and making timely submissions once the extension period begins. By prioritizing accuracy and transparency, your nonprofit can confidently meet its compliance obligations and continue building trust with its stakeholders.

Acknowledging Donor Contributions

Saying "thank you" isn't just polite—it's essential for compliance and donor relations. Sending prompt acknowledgment letters shows donors their impact and satisfies IRS regulations for tax deductions. For donations of $250 or more, you're required to provide a written acknowledgment, though it's a best practice to acknowledge every gift, no matter the amount.

A strong acknowledgment letter starts with a personal touch. Use the donor's name and reference the date and amount of the donation. Explain how their contribution makes a difference, whether it's funding a specific program or supporting the overall mission. Transparency is crucial—if no goods or services were exchanged for the gift, explicitly state that in the letter. Include your organization's name, EIN, and a leader's signature for authenticity.

Here's an example of how your letter might read:

[Your Organization's Letterhead]
[Date]
[Donor's Name]
[Donor's Address]

Subject: Thank You for Your Generous Donation

Dear [Donor's Name],

Thank you for your generous contribution of [Amount] on [Date]. Your support allows us to [impact statement—like provide meals, fund scholarships, or build housing].

No goods or services were provided in exchange for this donation, making it fully tax-deductible under IRS guidelines. Our federal EIN is [EIN].

Your kindness fuels our mission, and we're grateful to have you as a partner in this work.

Warm regards,
[Executive Director's Name]
[Title]
[Organization's Name]

While formal acknowledgment letters are essential for larger donations, smaller contributions should not go unnoticed. A simple yet effective receipt can be enough to confirm the donation and assure the donor that their generosity is recognized. This receipt should clearly outline key details such as the organization's name, Employer Identification Number (EIN), date of contribution, and the amount donated.

Leveraging automation tools and templates can streamline this process, ensuring that every donor—regardless of the size of their gift—receives timely and consistent acknowledgment. By maintaining a standardized yet personal approach, nonprofits can cultivate trust and encourage continued support, making donors feel valued and appreciated for their contributions to the mission.

Creating an Annual Report That Engages

Your annual report is more than just a compliance document—it's a powerful narrative that encapsulates the heart of your nonprofit's journey over the past year. It's an opportunity to share the triumphs and challenges, highlight the impact you've made, and invite stakeholders into the ongoing story of your mission. By crafting an engaging and well-structured report, you ensure that donors, partners, and community members see the depth and significance of your work.

A compelling annual report begins with a heartfelt message from leadership. Whether it's a letter from the executive director or board chair, this introduction sets the tone, providing a reflective look at the organization's milestones and aspirations for the future. It's a chance to reaffirm your nonprofit's mission and values, reminding readers why your work matters and why their support is crucial.

Beyond the numbers and compliance details, your annual report should serve as a bridge—connecting stakeholders to the real, human stories behind your mission. Through thoughtful storytelling, impactful visuals, and clear financial transparency, your nonprofit can turn an annual obligation into a powerful tool for inspiration and engagement.

The heart of the annual report lies in its impact narrative—the story of your nonprofit's journey over the past year, brought to life through the voices of those you serve. A well-crafted impact narrative does more than just present numbers; it connects readers emotionally to your mission, making them feel the significance of the work being done.

To create an engaging and meaningful impact narrative, use clear and evocative language that paints a vivid picture of transformation. Instead of simply stating statistics, illustrate their meaning through compelling stories from beneficiaries. Feature testimonials from those who have been directly affected by your programs, showcasing the tangible ways in which your organization has changed lives. Support these stories with visuals—infographics that break down key metrics, photographs that capture real moments of impact, and quotes from stakeholders that reflect the heart of your mission.

Numbers also play an essential role in reinforcing your story. Rather than listing data in isolation, frame them in context: How many meals were served, and what did that mean for families struggling with food insecurity? How many people found housing, and how did it impact their quality of life? How many scholarships were awarded, and what doors did they open for recipients? Providing this deeper context allows stakeholders to see the true value of your work and inspires them to remain engaged with your cause.

By weaving together compelling storytelling, striking visuals, and meaningful data, your impact narrative transforms your annual report from a compliance document into a powerful testament to your nonprofit's mission and the difference it is making in the world.

Financial transparency is the cornerstone of stakeholder trust, making it essential to provide a comprehensive and engaging financial summary in your annual report. Rather than just listing numbers, use this opportunity to tell the story behind your financials—how donor contributions and funding sources have fueled your mission and made an impact throughout the year.

Break down your revenues and expenses in a way that is easy to understand, using charts and visuals to illustrate how funds were allocated to different programs and initiatives. Highlight key financial achievements, such as securing new grants, increasing operational efficiency, or expanding services due to improved funding.

Beyond the numbers, take a moment to celebrate the generosity and commitment of those who made your work possible. Recognize key donors, sponsors, and volunteers—not just as contributors but as partners in your mission. Share testimonials or stories about how their involvement has helped drive success. By weaving in gratitude and context alongside financial details, you create a narrative that resonates with stakeholders and reinforces their confidence in your organization's stewardship of resources.

As you conclude your annual report, extend a heartfelt invitation for your readers to become active participants in your mission. Encourage them to take the next step— whether through a financial contribution, volunteering their time, or using their voice to advocate for your cause. Let them know that their involvement, no matter the form, is invaluable and that they are a vital part of the impact your organization creates.

Make this transition seamless by providing clear and accessible ways for them to engage. Include a direct link or QR code for donations, highlight upcoming volunteer opportunities, and offer suggestions on how they can champion your mission in their own communities. By making it easy and inspiring for them to act, you create a lasting connection that transforms supporters into dedicated partners in your nonprofit's journey.

Structure of an Annual Report

1. **Cover Page**: A bold image and engaging title.

2. **Table of Contents**: Clear navigation to each section.

3. **Letter from Leadership**: Message from the executive director or board chair.

4. **Year in Review**: Major milestones and impact stories.

5. **Financial Summary**: Revenue, expenses, and program allocation.

6. **Donor and Volunteer Recognition**: Celebrate key supporters.

7. **Call-to-Action**: Encourage readers to stay involved.

8. **Back Cover**: Contact information and social media links.

Your annual report is more than just a document—it is a reflection of your nonprofit's journey, an opportunity to celebrate the progress made, and a tool to inspire continued engagement. Through a blend of thoughtful design, compelling storytelling, and transparent reporting, your annual report becomes a powerful piece that resonates with your stakeholders, leaving a lasting impression.

By mastering these three core pillars of compliance—filing IRS Form 990, acknowledging donors with gratitude, and crafting an engaging annual report—your nonprofit does more than meet legal obligations. You cultivate trust with funders, energize supporters, and solidify your organization's place as a responsible and effective force for good. When these elements come together seamlessly, they do more than inform—they inspire action, rallying a community around your mission and setting the foundation for sustained growth and impact in the years to come.

Scaling and Sustaining Your Nonprofit

Every nonprofit founder begins their journey with a dream— a vision of creating meaningful change in the world. In those early days, it often feels like a race against time, scrambling to get programs off the ground, forging connections with potential supporters, and securing enough funding to keep the doors open. These moments are filled with passion, but they also come with immense pressure. The question that looms in every founder's mind isn't just how to start, but how to build something that lasts.

Yet, true impact isn't measured by surviving the first year. It's about moving beyond mere survival and into a space of growth and sustainability. A successful nonprofit doesn't just react to challenges; it plans ahead, builds strong foundations, and scales in a way that strengthens its mission rather than diluting it. Growth should be intentional, with careful thought given to when and how to expand, how to establish financial stability, and how to prepare for the future.

This chapter will take you beyond the startup phase, diving into the core strategies that will help your nonprofit not only survive but thrive. You'll learn how to assess the right moments for expansion, build reserves to safeguard against financial downturns, and create a roadmap that ensures your organization is positioned for lasting success.

When to Expand: When and How to Grow Your Team, Programs, or Funding

Growth can feel exhilarating—like stepping onto a high-speed train toward greater impact—but it can also be daunting. Expand too soon, and you risk spreading your resources too thin, leaving your team overworked and your finances precarious. Wait too long, and you may find yourself struggling to meet growing community needs, missing opportunities to deepen your impact. So how do you know when the time is right to scale? Think of it like tending a garden. A gardener doesn't simply scatter seeds and hope for the best. They prepare the soil, ensure there's adequate water and sunlight, and remain attentive to weather patterns. Similarly, nonprofits must be intentional about growth, carefully evaluating their internal capacity, funding sustainability, and alignment with their mission. Just as a garden flourishes with the right balance of preparation and care, a nonprofit thrives when it expands thoughtfully, with strong foundations in place to support its growth.

When to Expand

- **Mission Demand:** Picture this: You manage a food pantry that has long been a pillar of support for struggling families. Every week, more individuals arrive, hoping to receive essential groceries, but your shelves are growing emptier by the day. The line outside your door stretches farther than it ever has before, and you start noticing that some families are leaving empty-handed. Volunteers work tirelessly to meet the need, yet there simply isn't enough food, funding, or space to keep up with demand. In this moment, you realize that expansion is not just an option—it's a necessity. When the community's reliance on your services exceeds your current capacity, it becomes a pivotal moment to assess how growth can better fulfill your mission and ensure no one is turned away.

- **Financial Readiness:** Before you take the leap into hiring new staff or expanding your programs, take a moment to assess your financial foundation. Imagine standing at the edge of a canyon, preparing to cross to the other side. Do you have a sturdy bridge, or are you stepping onto shaky ground? Expansion requires stability. Examine your funding streams carefully—do you have reliable, recurring revenue that can support new initiatives, or are you relying on a one-time grant that might not be renewed? Diversified income sources, such as donor contributions, grants, earned revenue, and corporate partnerships, can provide a cushion against financial instability. It's also essential to project your future financial needs. If you hire additional staff, will you be able to sustain their salaries a year from now? If you launch a new program, will you have the operational funds to keep it running beyond the initial excitement? Taking the time to assess financial readiness will help ensure that your nonprofit grows strategically, avoiding pitfalls that could compromise its mission in the long run.

- **Operational Capacity:** Imagine your nonprofit as a bustling kitchen during peak hours—staff hurrying between stations, ingredients running low, and orders piling up. If your kitchen is too small or your team too overwhelmed, the quality of the food suffers, no matter how delicious the recipe. The same is true for your nonprofit. Before you grow, take a hard look at your operational infrastructure. Do you have enough skilled team members to manage the increased workload? Are your processes efficient, or do bottlenecks slow everything down? Is your technology outdated, making collaboration and data tracking more of a headache than a help? Expansion without a strong foundation is like adding floors to a house without reinforcing the beams below. If your current structure can't support the weight, everything risks collapsing under pressure. Thoughtful scaling requires investing in systems, training, and tools that create a stable platform for growth, ensuring that as you expand, your organization remains strong, resilient, and capable of delivering on its mission with excellence.

- **Strategic Alignment:** Growth is exciting, but it should always serve your nonprofit's core purpose. Imagine a lighthouse guiding ships safely to shore— its purpose is unwavering, despite the changing tides. Similarly, every expansion effort should be firmly rooted in your mission and long-term vision. It's easy to be tempted by new opportunities that seem promising, whether it's a potential grant that doesn't quite fit your programs or a partnership that requires shifting priorities. However, when you deviate from your mission, you risk diluting your impact and exhausting your resources on initiatives that do not serve your community in the way you originally intended. The best way to ensure strategic alignment is to ask: Does this expansion bring us closer to our mission? Does it reinforce the impact we set out to achieve? Staying disciplined in your growth choices will keep your nonprofit steady, effective, and deeply connected to the reason it was founded in the first place.

How to Expand

- **Team Growth:** Expanding your team is one of the most pivotal moments in your nonprofit's journey. It's not just about hiring—it's about finding the right people who align with your mission and will contribute meaningfully to the work ahead. Imagine building a house. You wouldn't just add rooms randomly; you would ensure that each addition has a purpose, fits structurally, and enhances the home's overall functionality. The same applies to your team. Every new hire should be a thoughtful addition, reinforcing the strength and sustainability of your organization.

Do you need full-time employees who will immerse themselves fully in your organization's culture, growing alongside it for years to come? Or would part-time staff or contractors be a better fit, providing flexibility as your programs evolve? The answer isn't one-size-fits-all; it depends on the nature of your work, the funding you have available, and the specific expertise required at each stage of growth.

Hiring should be done with precision. Start by developing clear job descriptions that outline not just tasks, but the values and vision that guide your nonprofit. Prioritize candidates who share your passion and commitment. If financial resources are tight, consider creative staffing solutions—part-time roles, shared positions with partner organizations, or engaging skilled volunteers for specialized projects.

Growth must be sustainable. Taking a phased approach—starting small, assessing impact, and gradually expanding—ensures that each new addition strengthens your nonprofit rather than straining its resources. By being intentional in your hiring process, you create a team that not only supports your mission today but lays the foundation for long-term success.

Think of hiring as an investment in your mission. Start by crafting clear job descriptions that not only outline responsibilities but also communicate your organization's values and expectations. Hiring with intention means seeking individuals who are not just skilled but also deeply committed to your cause.

If you're operating on a lean budget, consider starting with part-time or contract-based positions to manage workload without overwhelming your financial resources. You can also explore creative staffing solutions, such as shared positions with partner organizations or skilled volunteers who can fill gaps in expertise. Taking a phased approach to team expansion ensures that each new hire is sustainable and contributes to the long-term success of your nonprofit.

- **Program Growth:** Expanding a program isn't just about doing more—it's about doing better. Imagine you're running an after-school program that serves 50 children. The demand grows, and suddenly, you have the opportunity to serve 100. But before doubling capacity, you must ensure that the quality of education, mentorship, and engagement remains high. Can your staff handle the increase? Do you have the necessary funding, space, and resources to maintain the same level of excellence? Scaling should be a deliberate process, not a rushed reaction to demand. Instead of jumping in headfirst, consider piloting small expansions. Try adding 10 more participants before taking on 50, or extending program hours before launching a whole new initiative. This phased approach allows you to evaluate impact, troubleshoot challenges, and refine your strategies, ensuring that growth strengthens your mission rather than stretching your organization too thin.

- **Funding Growth:** Money fuels growth, but not all funding is created equal. The temptation to pursue every available grant or donation can be strong, but without careful consideration, this approach can pull your nonprofit in too many directions, leading to mission drift. Imagine a tree spreading its roots too thin—it may grow quickly, but without deep, strong roots in nourishing soil, it risks toppling over in the face of a storm. Instead of chasing every dollar, focus on cultivating long-term relationships with funders who align with your mission and share your vision for impact. This means developing trust, demonstrating accountability, and ensuring that funders see themselves as partners in your work rather than just financial backers. Additionally, diversifying revenue streams is crucial for stability. A healthy mix of grants, individual donors, corporate sponsorships, and earned income can ensure that your nonprofit isn't overly dependent on any single source of funding. Thoughtful financial planning and relationship-building will provide the strong foundation needed for sustainable, mission-driven growth.

- **Technology and Systems:** Imagine trying to run a marathon in worn-out shoes—your progress is hindered, and every step becomes more exhausting than the last. The same applies to growing a nonprofit without the right technology and systems in place. As your organization expands, so do the complexities of managing donor relationships, tracking finances, and streamlining operations. Investing in a robust donor management system ensures that your relationships with supporters remain strong and well-documented, while upgrading financial software keeps your accounting accurate and transparent. Growth without efficient systems is like adding weight to an already heavy load—eventually, it leads to burnout. By prioritizing the right tools and processes, your nonprofit can scale with confidence, allowing your team to focus on the mission rather than getting bogged down by inefficiencies.

Building Reserves: How to Prepare for Financial Slowdowns or Emergencies

Every nonprofit will face financial challenges. It's not a matter of "if" — it's "when." Picture this: you've worked tirelessly to secure funding, carefully budgeting every dollar to support your mission. Then, without warning, a major grant payment is delayed. Payroll is due, program costs are mounting, and the pressure to keep things running smoothly is immense. Without reserves, you're left scrambling—calling funders, shifting budgets, and possibly making tough decisions that could impact your team and the community you serve. But with a reserve fund in place, you can breathe easier, knowing you have a financial cushion to weather unexpected disruptions. This section will guide you through building that safety net, ensuring your nonprofit remains resilient and prepared for whatever challenges come your way.

What Are Reserves?

Reserves are your nonprofit's financial safety net, a cushion that protects your mission when the unexpected strikes. Imagine running a community program that hundreds rely on, and suddenly, a key grant is delayed or donor contributions decline. Without reserves, you're faced with difficult choices—scaling back services, reducing staff hours, or even shutting down crucial programs. But with a healthy reserve fund, you have breathing room, allowing you to navigate financial uncertainties without making drastic cuts. These funds ensure that no matter the challenges ahead, your organization can continue its work, keeping stability and impact at the forefront.

How Much Should You Have in Reserves?

The common rule is to have 3 to 6 months of operating expenses saved. This isn't a "nice to have" — it's essential for stability. Think about your rent, payroll, utilities, and other critical expenses. If your monthly operating cost is $20,000, aim to have $60,000 to $120,000 in reserves.

How to Build Reserves

- **Start Small:** Building a reserve fund doesn't require a sudden windfall or a drastic budget shift. Think of it like filling a jar with spare change—it may seem insignificant at first, but over time, those small contributions add up to something substantial. Start by allocating just a small percentage of your unrestricted funds each year. Even setting aside 5% consistently can create a meaningful cushion over time. The key is consistency—treating savings as an essential expense rather than an afterthought. As your nonprofit grows, so too will your reserves, ensuring that when financial challenges arise, you have the security to navigate them without compromising your mission.

- **Seek Unrestricted Funding:** Not all grants are created equal. Some come with tight restrictions, dictating exactly how and where the money must be spent, which can leave little room for flexibility. However, others provide unrestricted funding, giving your nonprofit the freedom to allocate resources where they are most needed—whether it's keeping the lights on, investing in staff development, or expanding a critical program. Think of it as the difference between a gift card to a single store versus a check you can use anywhere. The key is to actively seek funders who understand the importance of operational sustainability and trust your organization to use their contributions wisely. Building relationships with these funders not only strengthens financial stability but also fosters long-term partnerships that can support your mission beyond just one grant cycle.

- **Invest Wisely:** Having reserves is one thing, but making them work for you is another. Think of your reserves as a garden—you wouldn't just let the soil sit untouched; you'd plant seeds, nurture them, and watch them grow. The same principle applies to financial stewardship. If your nonprofit has significant reserves, consider placing them in safe, low-risk investments that generate modest returns while preserving capital. Options like high-yield savings accounts, money market funds, or conservative investment portfolios can help your organization's financial cushion grow steadily over time. However, investment decisions should align with your risk tolerance and long-term sustainability goals. Work closely with financial advisors or your board to create an investment strategy that balances growth with security, ensuring your nonprofit remains financially resilient for years to come.

- **Create a Board Policy:** Establishing a strong financial foundation requires more than just setting money aside—it demands a structured, well-defined plan. Work closely with your board to craft a comprehensive "Reserve Policy" that not only outlines how much should be saved but also clarifies the conditions under which these funds can be accessed. Consider the long-term sustainability of your organization by defining the specific steps for replenishing reserves after they are used. This policy should serve as a guiding document, ensuring that financial stability remains a priority and that reserves are used strategically to protect and strengthen your nonprofit's mission. By embedding these safeguards, you empower your organization to navigate financial uncertainties with confidence and resilience.

When to Use Reserves

Reserves are like a nonprofit's lifeline, meant for true emergencies rather than routine cash flow fluctuations. Picture them as a fire extinguisher—you don't reach for it unless there's a real fire threatening your stability. These funds should be used strategically, ensuring that when unexpected challenges arise, your organization has the financial strength to weather the storm without compromising its mission. Here's when it's appropriate to dip into them:

- The grant you were counting on has been delayed, and payday is fast approaching. Your staff, the backbone of your mission, relies on their income, and the pressure mounts as you scramble to find a solution. Without reserves, you may have to make tough choices—cut back on programs, delay payments, or even consider layoffs. But with a financial cushion in place, you can weather this moment with confidence, ensuring your team stays focused on their work rather than worrying about their next paycheck.

- The economy takes a downturn, and suddenly, donor contributions start to dwindle. The once-reliable streams of support are drying up, leaving you scrambling to cover essential expenses. You see the impact in real-time—program budgets tightening, staff members growing anxious, and the community you serve depending on you more than ever. Without reserves, difficult decisions loom ahead—cutting back services, delaying payments, or even reducing staff. But with a well-prepared financial cushion, you can navigate these turbulent times with confidence, ensuring that your mission stays strong even when the financial landscape is uncertain.

- A sudden storm rolls through, leaving your community center with a leaky roof, or a vital piece of equipment breaks down right before a major event. These urgent, unforeseen expenses demand immediate attention, yet they often come with a hefty price tag. Without reserves, you might find yourself scrambling to find emergency funding, delaying critical repairs, or even putting programs on hold. However, with a well-prepared financial cushion, you can address these unexpected challenges swiftly and effectively, ensuring that your organization remains operational and continues to serve its mission without disruption.

Establishing a well-defined approval process with your board for accessing reserve funds is essential. Think of it as creating a roadmap for financial stability—one that ensures transparency, accountability, and strategic decision-making. Clearly outline the circumstances under which reserves can be used, who has the authority to approve withdrawals, and how funds will be replenished after use. This not only protects the long-term financial health of your organization but also reassures donors and stakeholders that reserves are being managed responsibly and with the mission in mind.

Long-Term Strategy: How to Think Beyond the First Year and Plan for Years 3-5

In the first year of running a nonprofit, survival is often the main focus. You're navigating challenges, securing funding, and working tirelessly to establish your programs. But true success isn't just about making it through year one—it's about laying the groundwork for a sustainable future. The real test of longevity comes in years three to five, when growth and sustainability move to the forefront. Without a strategic plan, many nonprofits find themselves in a constant state of reaction, always putting out fires rather than proactively building a solid foundation for the future. The key to long-term success is shifting from short-term survival to forward-thinking strategy. Let's explore how to make that transition effectively.

Why Long-Term Planning Matters

- **Stability:** A well-thought-out plan serves as an anchor, keeping your nonprofit steady even when unexpected storms arise. Whether it's the sudden loss of a major donor or an unplanned leadership transition, having a clear roadmap allows you to respond with confidence rather than panic. Instead of scrambling to fill funding gaps or reorganize on the fly, a strong strategic plan ensures that your nonprofit can weather uncertainties and continue making an impact without disruption.

- **Clarity:** Imagine a rowing team gliding across the water. If each rower paddles in a different direction, progress is slow, chaotic, and exhausting. But when everyone moves in unison, guided by a shared course, they propel forward with speed and efficiency. The same principle applies to your nonprofit. When your team has a clear vision of where the organization is headed, every decision, every action, and every effort is aligned toward a common goal. Clarity eliminates confusion, fosters collaboration, and ensures that every stakeholder—from staff to volunteers to board members—is working together with purpose, making the journey toward impact more effective and sustainable.

- **Donor Confidence:** Imagine a philanthropist deciding where to invest their charitable contributions. They're not just looking for a good cause; they want to support an organization with a clear plan for the future, one that demonstrates stability, transparency, and measurable impact. Funders want assurance that their contributions will be used effectively and that the nonprofit has a strategy for long-term sustainability. A well-articulated vision, strong financial management, and a history of success inspire confidence, making donors more likely to commit to ongoing support and larger investments in your mission.

What Should a 3-5 Year Plan Include?

- **Vision and Mission Alignment:** Your mission and vision serve as your nonprofit's guiding stars, illuminating the path forward even in times of uncertainty. Just as sailors rely on the North Star to navigate the vast ocean, your organization must consistently look to its mission and vision to steer its course. Reaffirming these core principles ensures that every decision—whether it's expanding programs, pursuing funding, or refining operations—stays aligned with your original purpose. Without this alignment, it's easy to drift, following opportunities that may seem beneficial but ultimately pull your organization away from its true impact. Take the time to revisit and refine your mission and vision regularly, ensuring they remain both relevant and inspiring for your team, stakeholders, and the communities you serve.

- **Strategic Goals:** Setting strategic goals is like plotting a course for a long journey—you need clear destinations to ensure your organization is moving forward with purpose. Identify 3-5 major goals that will propel your nonprofit toward sustainable growth, increased advocacy, stronger fundraising, or operational excellence. These goals should not only be ambitious but also actionable, providing a clear roadmap for progress. Whether it's expanding your programs to reach new communities, strengthening donor engagement, or developing internal systems for better efficiency, each goal should align with your mission and inspire collective action from your team and stakeholders.

- **Financial Projections:** Envisioning your nonprofit's financial future is like mapping out a long journey—you need to anticipate the resources required at each stage to ensure smooth travels. Estimating revenue and expenses for each year allows your organization to plan strategically, ensuring growth is sustainable rather than reactive. By forecasting funding streams, identifying potential shortfalls, and preparing contingency plans, you create a financial blueprint that helps your nonprofit remain resilient and adaptable. This forward-thinking approach not only strengthens decision-making but also builds confidence among donors, board members, and stakeholders who rely on your ability to manage finances effectively.

- **Team Development:** Just as a thriving garden requires careful cultivation, a nonprofit needs a deliberate strategy to nurture and develop its team. Hiring the right people at the right time is only part of the equation—true sustainability comes from fostering leadership, providing opportunities for growth, and ensuring institutional knowledge is passed along. Consider what your organization will need in three, five, or even ten years. Are you identifying potential leaders within your ranks? Are you investing in training and mentorship programs to strengthen your team's capabilities? Thoughtful team development not only prepares your organization for expansion but also empowers staff and volunteers to grow alongside your mission, ensuring a future that is as strong as its people.

- **Risk Assessment:** Running a nonprofit is much like sailing on open waters—calm days bring smooth progress, but unexpected storms can arise at any moment. To ensure long-term stability, it's crucial to identify potential threats before they become crises. One of the most common risks is grant dependence—relying too heavily on one funding source can leave an organization vulnerable if that funding suddenly disappears. But financial instability isn't the only challenge. Consider leadership transitions, shifts in public policy, economic downturns, or even reputational risks. By proactively assessing these vulnerabilities and creating contingency plans, your nonprofit can stay resilient, prepared to adjust course, and continue fulfilling its mission no matter what challenges arise.

How to Create a 3-5 Year Plan

- **Get Your Team Involved:** A nonprofit's strength lies in its people, and strategic planning is most effective when it's a collaborative effort. Engage your staff, board members, and stakeholders in meaningful discussions, ensuring that diverse perspectives shape the direction of your organization. By fostering an inclusive planning process, you create a sense of ownership and shared commitment, empowering everyone to contribute their expertise and passion. Whether through brainstorming sessions, strategic retreats, or structured feedback loops, involving your team early and often ensures that your long-term vision is both ambitious and achievable.

- **Use SMARTIE Goals:** Setting goals isn't just about checking boxes—it's about creating a vision for success that is clear, actionable, and inclusive. Your goals should be **Specific**, defining exactly what you aim to achieve. They should be **Measurable**, ensuring progress can be tracked with concrete metrics. Goals should also be **Ambitious**, pushing your organization toward meaningful growth while remaining **Realistic**, acknowledging the resources and constraints you face. Establishing a **Time-bound** deadline keeps your team accountable, ensuring that progress doesn't stall. But beyond these traditional elements, your goals should also be **Inclusive**, ensuring that all voices, particularly those from marginalized communities, are considered in your planning. Finally, they must be **Equitable**, prioritizing fairness and justice in their implementation. By embracing SMARTIE goals, your nonprofit ensures that its objectives aren't just well-structured, but also deeply aligned with your mission and values.

- **Plan for Multiple Scenarios:** Just as a skilled sailor prepares for calm waters, sudden storms, and shifting winds, your nonprofit must anticipate various outcomes to remain resilient. Imagine the best-case scenario—your programs flourish, funding increases, and your team grows effortlessly. Now, picture the worst-case—a major donor pulls funding, economic conditions shift, or an unexpected crisis disrupts operations. The most-likely case often falls somewhere in between, requiring strategic adjustments along the way. By developing flexible, well-informed plans for each scenario, your nonprofit can adapt swiftly, minimize risks, and continue fulfilling its mission no matter what challenges arise.

Keeping the Plan Alive

A strategic plan is not meant to be a forgotten document tucked away in a file—it should be a living, breathing roadmap that guides your nonprofit's journey. Infuse it into your daily operations, use it as a compass during board meetings, and revisit it regularly to ensure it remains relevant. A strong plan adapts to change and evolves alongside your organization, helping you navigate challenges and seize opportunities. By reviewing and refining it quarterly, you ensure that it remains a tool for progress rather than a relic of past intentions. You're not just writing a plan—you're architecting the future of your nonprofit.

Scaling and sustaining a nonprofit isn't about expansion for expansion's sake—it's about intentional, thoughtful growth that strengthens your mission rather than diluting it. Imagine your organization as a tree, deeply rooted in its values and steadily reaching toward new heights. Growth should come at the right time, with the right support, ensuring your foundation remains strong. By recognizing the right moments to expand, cultivating financial stability, and crafting a vision that extends years into the future, you create the conditions for lasting impact. Stay deliberate, let your mission guide every decision, and nurture your nonprofit's potential. With patience and strategic planning, your organization will not only survive but flourish for generations to come.

Conclusion

Starting a nonprofit organization is one of the most rewarding journeys you can undertake. It is a path marked by passion, perseverance, and an unyielding commitment to making a positive impact in the world. While the road is undoubtedly challenging, it is equally transformative. This journey requires you to wear many hats—visionary leader, legal expert, fundraiser, operations manager, and community advocate—sometimes all at once. But with the right preparation, mindset, and support, you can build an organization that not only survives but thrives.

This book has provided a step-by-step guide to help you navigate the complexities of nonprofit creation. From defining your mission and securing your legal status to building a board, raising funds, and managing day-to-day operations, each chapter has been designed to equip you with the tools, insights, and strategies needed to succeed. The aim has been to demystify the process and present it in a way that is accessible, practical, and actionable.

By now, you've learned that starting a nonprofit goes far beyond filling out forms and meeting regulatory requirements. It's about building something that endures. It's about creating a legacy of service, equity, and transformation. You've also seen that this work is deeply relational—whether you're recruiting a board, engaging donors, or connecting with the community you aim to serve. People are at the heart of every successful nonprofit.

As you move forward, remember these key takeaways:

1. **Stay Grounded in Your Mission**: Your mission is your north star. Let it guide every decision you make, from strategic planning to daily operations. When challenges arise—and they will—your mission will remind you why you started.

2. **Prioritize Financial Stewardship**: Nonprofit status does not mean 'no profit.' It means responsible financial management that serves your mission. Create strong financial policies, build diverse revenue streams, and practice transparency with donors and stakeholders.

3. **Invest in People and Relationships**: Your board, staff, volunteers, and supporters are your most valuable assets. Take time to cultivate relationships, communicate regularly, and foster a culture of inclusion and accountability.

4. **Embrace Continuous Learning and Adaptation**: The nonprofit landscape is always evolving. Be ready to adapt, learn from mistakes, and grow. Seek professional development opportunities for your team and stay informed on nonprofit best practices.

5. **Lead with Integrity and Accountability**: Trust is everything in the nonprofit world. Whether it's with funders, beneficiaries, or regulators, your integrity is your reputation. Commit to transparency, ethical decision-making, and accountability in all you do.

As you take your first steps toward founding your nonprofit, know that you are not alone. Many have walked this path before you, and many will walk it after you. You're joining a powerful movement of people dedicated to advancing causes that matter. Leverage the resources, networks, and wisdom of those who have gone before you. Reach out for mentorship, connect with nonprofit associations, and be willing to share your story with others.

Remember, too, that perfection is not the goal—progress is. Each action you take, each hurdle you overcome, and each life you impact is a step toward fulfilling your mission. There will be setbacks, but there will also be victories that remind you of the power of perseverance.

Your nonprofit's success will not be measured solely by the number of grants you win or the size of your annual budget. It will be measured by the lives you touch, the communities you strengthen, and the justice you promote. Stay focused on that impact, and you will leave a lasting legacy.

In closing, let this be your call to action. You have everything you need to start your nonprofit: the vision, the knowledge, and the drive. Lean into your passion, seek guidance when needed, and celebrate every milestone along the way. Your work will matter—not just to those you serve but to the broader world that needs your leadership, courage, and compassion.

So go ahead. File your paperwork. Build your board. Craft your fundraising pitch. Launch your first program. The world is waiting for your vision, your passion, and your determination to make a difference.

With every policy you write, every story you tell, and every impact you create, you'll be building something far bigger than an organization—you'll be building hope. And in a world that often seems divided, hope is the most precious gift of all.

Thank you for embarking on this journey, and thank you for the work you're about to do. May it inspire others, just as you have been inspired to start.

With gratitude and encouragement,

Matthew B. Scraper

Glossary of Nonprofit Terms

Understanding nonprofit language is essential for navigating the sector with confidence. Below are key terms that are frequently used in nonprofit operations, governance, and development.

1. **501(c)(3)** - A section of the Internal Revenue Code (IRC) that designates an organization as tax-exempt for charitable, religious, educational, scientific, and certain other purposes.

2. **501(c)(4)** - A section of the IRC that designates an organization as tax-exempt for social welfare purposes, often allowing more political lobbying than a 501(c)(3).

3. **Annual Fund** - A nonprofit's campaign to raise funds on a recurring basis, typically every year, to support operational expenses and general programming.

4. **Board of Directors** - The governing body responsible for overseeing the strategic direction, financial health, and legal compliance of the organization.

5. **Bylaws** - The internal rules that govern how a nonprofit operates, including processes for board meetings, elections, and decision-making.

6. **Capacity Building** - Efforts to strengthen an organization's effectiveness, sustainability, and ability to fulfill its mission.

7. **Conflict of Interest** - A situation in which a person's private interests could interfere with their official duties for the organization.

8. **Donor-Advised Fund (DAF)** - A charitable investment account that allows donors to make contributions, receive immediate tax benefits, and recommend grants over time.

9. **Executive Director (ED)** - The highest-ranking staff member in many nonprofits, responsible for day-to-day operations and implementing the board's strategic vision.

10. **Fiscal Sponsorship** - A formal arrangement in which a nonprofit organization sponsors a project that may not have its own tax-exempt status.

11. **Form 990** - An annual tax form that most tax-exempt organizations must file with the IRS, providing transparency on financials, activities, and governance.

12. **Grant** - A financial donation made to a nonprofit organization to support a specific project, program, or general operating expenses.

13. **Logic Model** - A tool that outlines the relationship between a nonprofit's resources, activities, outputs, and intended outcomes.

14. **Mission Statement** - A formal statement that defines the organization's purpose, goals, and core values.

15. **Nonprofit Organization (NPO)** - An organization that operates for public benefit, rather than for profit, and is often eligible for tax-exempt status under the IRC.

16. **Program-Related Investment (PRI)** - Investments made by foundations to support charitable activities that may generate returns.

17. **Restricted Funds** - Donations or grants that are limited to specific uses, as stipulated by the donor.

18. **Stakeholder** - Any individual, group, or entity affected by or invested in the nonprofit's activities, such as donors, volunteers, staff, and community members.

19. **Strategic Plan** - A document outlining the organization's long-term goals and strategies for achieving its mission.

20. **Unrestricted Funds** - Funds that are not tied to a specific purpose and can be used at the nonprofit's discretion.

This glossary serves as a foundation for deeper understanding as you navigate nonprofit operations and strategy.

Recommended Reading

Books, articles, and resources that can further your knowledge of nonprofit leadership, governance, and operational excellence.

By Matthew B. Scraper

7. Effective Nonprofit Board Governance: Roles, Responsibilities, and Best Practices for Committees and Directors

8. From the Pulpit to the Boardroom: How I Transitioned from a 20-Year Career in Ministry to the Nonprofit Sector

9. Policies and Procedures for Nonprofit Success: A Comprehensive Guide to Ethical and Effective Governance

10. The Nonprofit Operations Playbook: Strategic Operations for Mission-Driven Organizations

11. How to Start a Nonprofit (and Actually Succeed!): A Step-by-Step Guide for Visionaries and Changemakers

12. The Nonprofit Project Management Handbook: Deliver Projects that Drive Nonprofit Impact

13. Strategic and Tactical Planning for Nonprofits and Churches: A How-To Guide for Visionaries and Leaders

Online Resources

1. Free Templates and other resources at: https://mbsoperations.com/free-resources

2. **National Council of Nonprofits** — A go-to resource for trends, best practices, and policy updates impacting nonprofits.

3. **Foundation Center (now Candid)** — Offers resources on grantmaking foundations, proposal writing, and fundraising.

4. **Grantspace** — Provides learning resources for nonprofits seeking grants and funding.

5. **BoardSource** — A nonprofit that provides leadership resources and training for nonprofit board members.

These books, guides, and resources will help you deepen your understanding of nonprofit best practices, enhance your leadership skills, and strengthen your organization's impact.